The Magic Within

The Magic Within

Simple Ways to Raise Your Vibrations

Kara Evans & Britt Schelling

Evans & Schelling Publishing

ISBN: 979-8-218-10227-2

Edited by Larry Butler, Kristin Campbell
Cover design by Wonderbug Creations
Vectors by RawPixel.com
Interior formatting by Britt Schelling

This book is intended as general information only and should not be used to diagnose or treat any health condition or replace the advice of a trained medical professional. The information given here is designed to help you make informed decisions about your spiritual health. It is not intended as a substitute for any treatment that may have been prescribed by your physician. If you suspect that you have a medical condition, we urge you to seek competent medical attention.

The names used in illustrative examples in this book, except those of the authors themselves, have been changed to respect and protect the identities of the parties involved.

Evans & Schelling Publishing
magicwithinbook@gmail.com

To our families, of both blood and soul, we honor you with the lessons you've helped us discover.

CONTENTS ▌

DEDICATION   v
PREFACE   ix
INTRODUCTION   xi

One ▌ LEVERAGE YOUR FEARS   1

Two ▌ DISCOVER YOUR SELF   19

Three ▌ MANIFEST YOUR DESIRES   35

Four ▌ LOVE YOUR LIFE   51

Five ▌ HONOR YOUR JOURNEY   65

Six ▌ NOTICE YOUR MAGIC   77

Seven ▌ TRUST YOUR SOURCE   91

CONCLUSION   105
ACKNOWLEDGMENTS   107
TO OUR FAMILIES   109
ABOUT THE AUTHORS   111

The genesis of *The Magic Within* began as a quick spark of an idea. As Kara was cutting her grass in May 2022, she received a strong psychic download to write a book with Britt, an acquaintance from the community. Kara trusted her gut and instantly called Britt to explain.

Britt, a lifelong writer who had yet to take the leap to published author, surprised herself by saying without hesitation, "Definitely. Let's do this."

From that point, Kara and Britt flowed with forward motion, utilizing ease, not speed. They planned, discussed, and drafted. Content poured from their hearts, inspired by insights they'd encountered and practices they'd developed throughout their lives. They compromised, shared workloads, and showed up for crack-of-dawn work sessions before their "actual responsibilities" began. Through scheduled obligations, family demands, extra hours, and even one grueling first trimester, they preserved and produced.

Without opening to the signs, answering the call, and following their Inner Knowing, this book would cease to exist. *The Magic Within* is a dream made manifest, and ultimately, it was created for you.

Inhale. Take a deep breath. Listen closely.

You, my dear, are magic.

You have intuitive faculties beyond your wildest dreams.

Being intuitive is experiencing a *knowing*. It's seeing and comprehending the signs around you, trusting the visceral gut feeling deep inside, and becoming one with your Higher Source. Within you exists an entire universe of possibility.

Each of us has innate abilities, and the world is waiting for us to tap into our full potential.

It all starts with picking up this book. Today is the day that you level up with higher vibrations. It's time to unleash *The Magic Within*.

Among these pages, you'll learn how to open your heart, assert your magical self, implement instant mindset shifts, and strengthen your spiritual skillset. These exercises require mere moments of your time, cost no money, and call for only your focus and belief.

We don't aim to change you – *you don't need to change!* – we simply offer a path to an upgrade so you can start living from a space of manifesting what you *want* instead of what you *don't want.*

In *The Magic Within*, you'll discover that you've never been lost (even if you've felt that way for a while), and you're certainly not alone. You'll dive into stories that you may recognize as your own. You may already know this material; if so, consider this text a cosmic reminder. Take from it what you want and leave the rest. Let this book be a vibrational lifeline back home that connects you to everyone and everything else.

And in those moments when our minds feel as if they're fraying with the blackness of depression or spiraling out of control with anxiety, we may decide to supplement with material-world help: therapy, rehabilitation programs, support groups, medication, etc. That's how it is. Simply that. And we never pass judgment on another's journey.

The Magic Within was written for everyone. It's a metaphorical hug for the soul and a high-five for the spirit.

As authors, we want you to see us for who we are: two women who raise our vibrations to create our most radical lives, lives that are very different and continue to take very diverse paths. We're simply figuring out this wild, wild world as we go, but we've learned how to hone our Inner Knowing along the way. *The Magic Within* is an expression of our servant hearts.

A kind disclaimer: Throughout this text, we use the terms *Inner Light, Inner Voice, Inner Knowing,* and *Higher Self.* You might replace these terms with *God* or *Goddess, Spirit Guides, the Universe, the Natural Order, the Cosmos, the Unconscious*, etc. If you feel called to make this change, please do. We honor your spirituality and stand behind your personal beliefs.

The Magic Within reinforces that *knowing*, whatever that *knowing* means to you. It is within your own heart that you find this answer, and the path you feel guided to follow is your choice alone. However you experience your spirituality, remember that it emanates through you.

You are human. You are divine. You are magic.

You are so much more powerful than you realize.

With all the love in the universe,

Kara and Britt

One

LEVERAGE YOUR FEARS

All that you need is within you at this very moment. Ground your-self and settle into your sacred space. From there, change your thoughts to change your life.

TAKE A MOMENT TO SIMPLY *BE*

It's amazing to consider the potential that's within reach right now. But we're casting it aside in favor of so-called responsibilities, societal ideals, and the constant pressure of doing, doing, doing.

The world may seem like it's turning in unruly measures, but you don't have to commit to the chaos. Just sit with yourself for a moment. What will benefit you most is knowing firsthand that you can pause to breathe and life *will not fall apart*.

Release the need to *think*, much less *over*think.

In this momentary suspension exists an eternity: all that tran-spired to bring you here, all that occurs around you now, and all that you will eventually come to be. Absorb the energy from this space of understanding, and let it soothe your soul.

You're exactly where you're supposed to be at the exact moment you're supposed to be here. The fact that you hold this book in your hands is no coincidence. You are intensely brave for briefly excusing yourself from your daily responsibilities on behalf of your spiritual development. Know this: you decide how you embrace life.

One of the most fulfilling ways to achieve clarity, stability, and mindfulness is to meditate. Meditation is a practice where we give ourselves full permission to *simply be*. We accept ourselves exactly as we are. We witness the miracle of life by being still.

There are countless ways to meditate, and each technique can be just as varied as the person meditating. To affirm your own personal agency, try this meditation for protection:

1. **Find a quiet space.** This can be anywhere. You can meditate on a yoga mat, under your bedroom comforter, in your car during your lunch break, etc.
2. **Pick a comfortable position.** Sit cross-legged on a pillow, rest in a chair, lie on the floor, etc.
3. **Steady your breathing.** For four counts each: exhale, hold, inhale, hold, and then start again. This technique utilizes a rhythmic pace. Cycle through this series for a minute or so, then return to your natural breathing pattern.
4. **Close your eyes and visualize.** Ask your Higher Source for protection and imagine beams of white light from the heavens as they enter your body through the top of your head, pulse down through your being, and shoot out through your

tailbone and/or feet. Those energy cords then wrap around the Earth's core, return through your body, and radiate from your crown and back into the skies above.

5. **Just be:** Take a few minutes to be with yourself. Thoughts will come but gently breathe through them and wisp them away with your exhale.

Meditation offers a precious pause, a baseline where we can recenter and recalibrate. We recommend taking a few moments for this exercise every day. Relaxation, awareness, and assurance are all benefits of a meditation session. When you quiet your mind, you'll cease the distraction and resistance of thought, and your vibrations will rise.

YOUR ENERGETIC VIBRATIONS

Everything is energy. And your energy is represented by vibrations. The frequency of those vibrations informs your reality as you perceive it to be.

Imagine your vibrations are represented by a thermometer. But instead of measuring temperature, this thermometer's scale indicates gradients of spiritual energy that span from "suffering" to "enlightened."

Our vibrations are these buzzing, charged, internal frequencies that express themselves through our emotional states.

When we're operating at higher vibrations, we feel lighter and healthier. We are in flow. We're breaking negative cycles and making choices that align with our desired lifestyles. Conversely, when operating at lower vibrations, we feel weighed down, stagnant, and sickly. We wallow in negativity. We focus on what we don't have, invent (or reinforce) our perceived limitations, and engage in self-destructive behavior.

Your vibrations affect your mindset; your mindset alters your perception of the world around you; your perception influences your behavior; your behavior sets the tone of your energetic exchange with others – and all over again. The rate of change can rapidly fluctuate as you expand and contract your energy.

But with exercise and awareness, we can willfully shift ourselves into an optimal state and establish our energetic baselines. When we alter our thoughts, we lift our conscious minds from misery, blame, hopelessness, and regret to places of clarity, happiness, simplicity, and peace.

By raising your vibrations, you can be a force of light! You can manifest positivity for yourself, which will radiate outward to all those around you. In turn, higher energetic levels from others will be welcomed and received by your open heart.

FEARS ARE FALLACIES

It is easier to be fearful than it is to be brave.

Each of us holds fear within us, and believe it or not, it has a beneficial place and purpose. As a survival tool, fear, at its most helpful, is an emotional response to valid forms of danger. Instinctively, we gravitate toward fear because it feels safer to contract than to expand.

However, some of us have an innate way of awfulizing everything and anything that could go wrong, resigning to the worst-case scenario, and scaring ourselves from experiencing the fullness of life.

- "Don't go there because it's dangerous."
- "Don't talk to them because they'll harm you."
- "Don't do that because you'll shame yourself."

Fear can disguise itself as control.

Interestingly enough, we're not controlling anything. Our limitations are in control by way of restraint and constraint. Fears become lies; untruths we allow ourselves to believe when they hold us back from the things we want in life.

Because you alone have given your fear power, only you can disarm it.

Fears are tricky and can stem from a variety of places – both from our own experiences and from the experiences of others. It is vital to deeply explore our fears to determine their origins, realistic threat levels, and likelihood of transpiring.

For instance, anytime you say "can't," dig deep to identify if you're experiencing a self-imposed limitation under the guise of fear.

- *"I can't* commit to one partner," might mean, *"I fear* I won't be able to connect wholeheartedly with one person because I don't know myself."
- *"I can't* leave my job," might mean, *"I fear* the unpredictability that occurs when I don't have steady income and benefits."

- *"I can't* publish my work," might mean, *"I fear* the public scrutiny that accompanies being seen for creative efforts."

Upon retrospect, you fear a possibility that's not predetermined to occur.

You're catastrophizing when you allow your fears to warp your perception of reality. Fixating on your fear becomes more treacherous than the fear itself. You identify with the fear; you may even become defensive of it, structuring your existence around the perpetual thought of it. You shift from "it may occur" to "it is bound to occur" to "it will occur with absolute certainty."

But in life, there are no absolutes.

Once you embrace your fears with curiosity, you may find that the weight of carrying the fear is much more daunting than the possibility of the fear happening. And even if that fear does occur, who is to say that the reality will be as bad as you expected it to be?

The thought of the fear is causing more suffering than the fear itself.

Feed your fear, and its force will smother you. But if you console your fear, invite its story to emerge, and dissect the myths, the lies will loosen their constricting grip on you. At the crossroads of fear and inquiry lies the path to unbridled freedom, ushering you toward unparalleled growth.

LEGACY FEARS

As you explore your fears, you may discover what you fear wasn't even your own to tackle. Fears can be passed down from generation to generation. Your legacy fear may have resulted from a negative experience endured by your guardian or another influential person in your life, and their modeled behaviors during your upbringing have passed along their fear to you.

For instance, one of Amy's earliest memories of stormy weather is being pulled from her bed at three a.m. by her mother, who would instruct the family to hunker down in a windowless hallway, lest they be struck by lightning. And to this day, Amy is an anxious mess every time the weatherperson predicts a downpour.

But amazingly, this particular fear of thunderstorms, now firmly set in Amy's psyche, predates any negative experience that Amy's known to have had with weather disturbances.

Amy approaches her fear with curiosity and recognizes that this assumed fear has permeated the three levels of her consciousness. She sees that, consciously, she is choosing fear-based behaviors, like structuring her schedule around weather reports. Subconsciously, this entrenched fear is emerging as a distressful emotional response. And unconsciously, Amy harbors a belief buried deep within, and she must investigate this linkage.

Upon exploration, Amy discovers that her mother, as a young child, underwent a harrowing incident during a violent thunderstorm while camping, in which she and her family were pulled from their collapsed pop-up by heroic strangers. This fear of thunderstorms, now operating through Amy from the unconscious level, is an extension of misplaced love, and at no point did Amy's mother wish to sabotage her daughter.

Armed with this greater understanding, Amy can now work to release this fear that she has claimed as her own for decades and effectively break the cycle for future generations.

That's right: Fear can be imparted *to* you out of protection *for* you. Trace your fears back to their root sources; your findings may shock *and* soothe you.

BABY STEPS TO BREAKTHROUGHS

Fears can be fantastic gifts because they highlight opportunities for evolution, and it's okay to unpack your fears slowly, with gratitude, respect, and understanding. Regardless of their sources, your fears can be used to your benefit.

For example, Emil finds himself thinking, *"I can't* lose this extra weight," but upon closer reflection, he identifies his fear and discovers, *"I fear* taking on such a painstaking goal because I've never been able to lose weight before."

It takes baby steps to build confidence. After all, movement starts with the will to walk. Babies crawl before they run. Stumbling comes before agility.

Using this slow-and-steady, step-by-step technique, Emil pledges himself to some "easy win," low-risk goals to build momentum: subscribing to a healthy meal service plan, completing a short-term exercise program, and connecting with like-minded friends who can help hold him accountable.

Emil opens to many options to readjust his relationship with his body while extending himself a compassionate lifeline should he "fall off the wagon." But, most importantly, Emil ritualizes recognition and celebration for every victory, no matter how small and insignificant they may seem. Eventually, the larger steps seem like easy upgrades because Emil has built the gradual momentum to propel himself onward.

It is possible that your fear, which is currently stunting your development, will seem like child's play in the future. So, flash forward to that frame of mind and take one small, shaky baby step immediately.

In fact, think about a time when you did something that scared you, a time you thought you wouldn't *survive*, yet you *thrived*.

Examples might include abrupt events: introducing yourself to someone who would eventually become your spouse, taking the chance on a new job, or extending a final goodbye to a terminally ill loved one. Other examples might include prolonged experiences: raising your children on a limited income, getting and staying sober, overcoming a debilitating injury, or paying down overwhelming debt.

In these examples, you thought you *couldn't*, but you *did*.

You've tackled the difficult. You've mounted the insurmountable. You have a proven history; a "Bravery Portfolio" of sorts. You're more than capable, and you'll be called to step forward again, and again, and again.

That's life. And that's growth. Life is growth. Muster your fortitude and commit to what's necessary – to both live *and* grow. Start small, and you'll eventually notice extraordinary changes.

FEEL THE FEELS, LOVE

And it happens! It's one of those moments where your perceived self-control has been torn asunder: you've had a loud, public disagreement with your mother-in-law; your kid throws a tantrum while getting a haircut; your boss accuses you of something you didn't do. You feel provoked, activated, and unable to reel reality back in.

What does a well-meaning friend say in an attempt to assuage you? They put their hands on your shoulders, look you straight in the eye, and loft those four holier-than-thou words: Take. A. Deep. Breath.

"What? I'm fine," you say defensively. "It's all fine. I don't need to breathe. See? I'm breathing right now?" Meanwhile, your hands tremble, a thumping emanates from your chest, and a drop of sweat weaves its way down your brow.

Few things can provoke a person more quickly than the diminutive phrase: Take a deep breath. Although seemingly innocuous, it's pithy and misguided. It endeavors to expedite us to a place of calmness, most likely for the benefit of the one who offered the directive.

So, instead of "Take a deep breath," we prefer **"Feel the feels, Love."**

The deluge of sentiments rushing toward you during these moments of emotional arousal don't need to be squelched; they need to be acknowledged. Then, ask yourself: **How can these thoughts serve me?**

From this space, and in your own good time, you can craft a response, not a reaction.

In the case of your child's unwanted public outburst at the salon, it might seem as if the child's meltdown set you off, spiraling you into a rage. However, it will serve you to stop, consider the situation, and identify the thoughts that ran through your mind just before you reacted. During self-reflection, you may realize that you were already stressing over having enough money to pay for your child's needs, and now you are feeling as if people are judging you poorly as a parent.

Wow! You know you're not a bad parent! You, my friend, have just unearthed an untruth that crept into your psyche and caused you to react. And the truth is that your child is only behaving as children sometimes do.

Shut down the lies, as only you can, and you'll experience peace. Plus, you'll be much more levelheaded and able to address your kiddo's big feelings.

Underlying stressors will often burst through any available pressure valve. If you feel activated, pinpoint what's going on in your life and use the tools you have to offer yourself grace. You're doing much, much better than you think you are.

THE CANCEL-THEN-CREATE METHOD

Your fears will continue to emerge and reemerge. Fear management is an active process. You'll encounter your fears again and again. You'll be called to evoke your firmness of character, and these repeated instances will build your self-assurance, making your courage easier and easier to access.

Each time you feel scared is yet another chance to prove *yourself* to *yourself*. When you experience a pervasively distressing, upending memory that's not serving you, replace it with something positive. Using the Cancel-then-Create method, you'll generate a much-needed shift in perspective.

This thought process is much like writing an email: You're typing on your computer, and you commit an error. Instantly, you use the delete button to make a correction. This all happens before you send the respective email to the intended party.

Along this same wavelength, we suggest altering a thought before transmitting it throughout the universe. The energy you emit will reflect your reality.

The Cancel-then-Create method works to redirect encoded information that tends to influence our perspective.

For example, John and his son engage in a disagreement. Reflecting on their rapport, John's mind instantly serves up another instance where his son retorted with backtalk and lost video game privileges. John then may lament over his perception of their "eroding" relationship, evidenced by this one obsessive thought, which stagnates as a contractive, heavier feeling throughout John's body.

However, instead of focusing on this particularly destructive memory, John can replace it with one that serves his soul and makes him feel content: a time when he and his smiling son were enjoying football on the beach. John then notices his body is lighter and more expansive, allowing him more control over his response and how he interacts with the world around him.

Alternatively, the Cancel-then-Create method helps us to address distress when the world requires us to stand by in discomfort.

For instance, a young pup was admitted for emergency surgery. Jack, her guardian, now waits apprehensively on updates from the veterinarian. Each time Jack senses an anxious thought, he visualizes pulling that particular worry from his mind, transforming it into an expression of love in the shape of a heart, and then sending it off to his canine best friend in intensive care.

How we communicate with ourselves matters. Our self-talk is the foundation that fortifies our self-perseverance.

Notice how a simple change in thought can expand you, serve you, and ultimately raise your vibrations. Observe your initial thoughts if you like, but don't automatically believe them. If fear is assaulting you with unhelpful information, use visualization to shift your awareness to the vibrational frequency that serves you best.

EARTH ANGELS

A professor encourages you to showcase your talent in an externship you hadn't considered: He's an Earth Angel. A friend takes an eight-hour bus ride to hug you deeply as you try to survive a difficult breakup: She's an Earth Angel. A fellow business owner emboldens you to develop a highly lucrative subset of your business: She's an Earth Angel.

An Earth Angel is a person who connects with you on an intense level, far past a run-of-the-mill friendship. Earth Angels make you feel special. They love you, accept you, and inspire you. With the gentlest guidance, they steer you from worrying about your worst because they believe in your best.

An Earth Angel offers you their time and wisdom. They reaffirm your reasons for being and help you to maximize your one precious life. Their goal is to nudge you toward your path of purpose and to help you safeguard against history repeating itself.

This is soul-satisfying work and, in partnership with you, your Earth Angel reinforces the life lessons they have learned, and they witness, through you, the birth of brilliance into the world. Oftentimes, your humble Earth Angel may not realize their importance, as your connection with one another is so natural.

A frantic search isn't necessary to identify an Earth Angel. They are already here. Just be willing to step outside your comfort zone and say "yes" to a chance that presents itself to you – you'll know when it feels right. And from that place, open your heart and prepare to receive.

Because the universal truth is this: you're already someone's Earth Angel, as well. It's time to do the arduous yet rewarding work of self-mastery and be ready to step forward and give yourself to another in need.

GROUND YOURSELF

Isn't it funny that being "grounded" was issued as punishment when we were children? When, all along, our well-meaning parents (albeit with faulty execution) were only trying to get us to level our energy.

Grounded, in the spiritual sense, is a state of balance between you and the natural world around you. It's when your energy and the Earth's energy are in equilibrium, or even exchange.

So, think about the times when everything seems to go wrong: You're running ten minutes behind. The kids aren't dressed yet and are stampeding around the house. You grab your cell phone, and it's dead. You can't find your keys to start the car. You search your purse and discover that applesauce has coated the interior lining. At that very second, a catapulted shoe knocks the contents of your bright purple smoothie onto your dry-cleaned shirt.

In overwhelming and emotionally-charged moments like these, when we scramble for sanity, we are juggling everything that's material yet affixing to nothing spiritual.

So, what do you do? **Drop. It. All.** Drop the commitments. Drop the expectations. Allow yourself to surrender to the moment, invite your feelings to wash over you, and remember – *all of this is temporary.*

Then claim an instant during the pandemonium and try one of these quick exercises to ground yourself in the goodness that supports you:

- **Savor a scent:** Crack open a bottle of your favorite essential oil and breathe it in deeply.
- **Use the bathroom:** Close the door and partake in one of the most intimate of human acts, reminding you that we're all on the same level.
- **Hold a piece of ice in your palm:** The jarringly cold temperature will restart your system with an unapologetic shock.
- **Recite a beloved poem:** Saying a quick poem, whether yours or another's, will act as an incantation to rise above the current chaos.
- **Assume Tree Pose:** In yoga, Tree Pose is standing tall, securing one foot to the floor, bringing the sole of your opposite foot to your standing leg, and reaching your arms high above, like a regal tree.
- **Touch a plant:** Commune with a flower and envision its stalk receiving your excess energy.
- **Be barefoot:** Stand on grass or bare ground outside and feel the Earth's magnetic pull.
- **Practice 5-4-3-2-1 meditation:** Be still. Notice five things you can see, four things you can hear, three things you can touch, two things you can smell, and one thing you can taste.
- **Visualize stability:** Imagine three cords, one from each foot and one from your tailbone, locking you into Mother Earth like the roots of a tree.

These represent only a handful of ways to ground yourself, but the possibilities are endless. You don't have to go to great lengths and engage in extravagant rituals. Stability can be asserted during any second of your existence. It may not always look pretty, but you'll feel slightly better. And again, you can set a higher initial threshold for yourself if you assert meditation as a daily practice.

By grounding yourself, you'll unearth a more clear, centered, and attuned self, anchoring to a little more steadiness in this unpredictable world.

LEVERAGE YOUR FEARS *Recap*

- *You're exactly where you're supposed to be at the exact moment you're supposed to be here.*
- *Spiritual vibrations are changeable internal frequencies that express themselves through our emotional states.*
- *Approach your fear with curiosity and diminish its power.*
- *That which you fear may have roots generations deep.*
- *Chip away at your fear with small actions, and your self-confidence will grow.*
- *Our feelings will reveal the true heart of the matter.*
- *When you experience a pervasive, distressful thought, replace it with something positive.*
- *Earth Angels support you and help you pursue your purpose.*
- *Ground yourself to put life into perspective and attune to the world around you.*

Two

DISCOVER YOUR SELF

Do you yearn to flourish, but instead, you languish in the same repeating routine? Well, it's time to meet and accept your authentic self! Because your relationship with your sense of self is the most important relationship you'll have in your lifetime.

EMBODY YOUR SPIRIT

It is vital to check in with your body. Physical sensations can be psychic signals within our bodies that serve as gateway points to deeper understanding. Allowing yourself to truly *feel* is to embody the physical sense of your existence.

Take a moment to check in with yourself. Use focused awareness to scan your body from head to toe. What sensory experiences are you observing and where?

You might identify physical sensations, such as muscle tension, a stomachache, tingling limbs, a racing heart, etc. You might unearth behavioral matters, such as difficulty concentrating, restlessness, moodiness, etc.

Now we would never suggest neglecting medical needs. It's important to develop open communication with health care professionals so that all concerns are discussed and underlying conditions are addressed.

However, it is worthwhile to consider that spiritual shifts may be evidenced by physical responses. Sensitivities can be the result of intuitive abilities.

Some cases in point:

- *Have your ears been ringing?* Listen closely. Your Inner Spirit may be sending a message to you.
- *Are you feeling lightheaded?* You may be intimately experiencing the energies around you.
- *Have you been choking on water?* Perhaps you need to speak your mind and share your truth.
- *Have rashes developed that come and go?* You may be detoxifying and releasing stagnancy surrounding psychic blockages.

Our bodies signal us. But if we're not paying attention and not making ourselves a priority, we'll never get the memo. Some of us are so numb, disassociated, and distracted that we can no longer link back to ourselves for genuine spiritual counsel.

The truth is, however, we expand into our *true knowing* when we release all that keeps us from *not feeling*. By allowing ourselves to feel, we experience life more deeply.

One exercise to honor your relationship with your body is to moisturize your skin with mindfulness. Choose your favorite body butter, and then apply it gently to your face, arms, and legs. Recognize your skin for what it is: the barrier between your inner and outer worlds. As you survey your skin, engage in a mental body scan. Acknowledge your body with appreciation. Offer homage to this awe-inspiring dermal frontier!

Experiencing sensations brings us back home to our bodies. And as you start to develop your intuition and shift into alignment, your physical and etheric selves become even more intertwined, building emotional resilience and reinforcing the concept that **everything – yes, everything – is connected.**

TRIGGERING OUR TRAUMAS

Grief is experienced as profound sadness due to loss: the end of a relationship, the death of a loved one, the depletion of vitality, the inability to manage affairs, or the failing of dreams and expectations.

Trauma is an intense emotional reaction that results from exposure to a tragic, sometimes life-threatening, incident. Although the experience that caused the torment is highly personal and will differ in scope, trauma is a pervasive universal occurrence. One may experience trauma through natural disasters, violence, abuse, and physical or emotional injury. Unprocessed trauma has lasting effects, trapping itself within the body, expressed as a stress response that affects one's self-view, physical well-being, relationships with others, and outlook on life.

Compounding trauma with grief may leave you feeling like a withered shell, a mere trace of the person you once were. Heart-wrenching hurt can leave one in an utter state of prolonged despair, often struggling to breathe, move, exist, feeling hollow to the core. To say you're "sad" fails to encompass the vast range of human experiences encapsulating this destabilizing condition.

We often attribute the suffering to the subject – the ex-husband, the life savings, the wasted youth – but it doesn't end there. What we're genuinely mourning is the loss of ourselves: the person we were, the life we had, the possibilities that had once been within reach. And in these moments of survival, it may feel as if healing is the furthest thing from our minds.

You may battle triggers, blaring mental alarms that abruptly shake awake a traumatic memory. Triggers can be words, topics, holidays, milestones, songs, smells, or anything that creates a sensory shortcut to recalled anguish. To an outsider, triggers may seem nonsensical; but to a survivor, triggers can cause a painful experience to resurface. Fireworks, for instance, while an exciting Fourth of July barbeque finale to some, can elicit utter distress in combat veterans. It is crucial to remain thoughtful, respectful, and understanding.

Triggers instantly disconnect us from our current lives. During these moments, remember that we are safe. We are not experiencing the same trauma. We are not in the same situation as we once were and are not obligated to summon emotional disturbances.

Empower yourself in the potentialities of the present.

Know this: You're not an issue that needs fixing, a problem that needs solving, or a disease that needs curing. You're a soul that needs healing. Healing is possible for everyone, and it's possible for you.

HEALING TAKES STRENGTH

When you speak of a traumatic event that you've experienced, you may lower your head and concede, "I feel like a part of me has died." And that's true. A version of you has verily met its end, especially in those heartbreaking situations where trauma has dissolved all sense of your identity.

Healing is the processing of painful life experiences, releasing expectations of what you believe your situation to be, and extending yourself permission to emerge renewed. The truth is, post-trauma, you'll never be the same person you once were. Emotional scars run much deeper than surface level, and you will remain altered forever, but **healing allows you to feel whole again.**

No matter the cause of the pain, *healing is possible*. But this work is not easy. It is up to you to determine when the time is right. You must *want* a life after healing. You must *explore* what scares you the most. You must *confront* your pain.

There are two components to healing: will and warmth. Through your will, you consciously *choose* to act. And through your warmth, you *follow through* with gentle, compassionate measures.

Unconditional love is checking in with yourself and asking: **How can I gently tend to my heart in this moment?**

As always, when you make an effort to activate your highest vibrations – no matter how sad or tired you may feel – the effects are dispersive. You're doing the best for yourself and everyone who touches your life.

True immersive, integrative healing takes time. It's not incremental. There is no continuum. It ebbs and flows. Healing processes may feel grueling and intense, but the work is worth it. The healing opportunities below are meant to meet you where you are, as you observe your emotions and nurture your well-being.

Use consideration to reach new levels of understanding. The woman in pajamas who failed to brush her hair that morning may have endured a miscarriage. The coworker with the vacant stare during meetings may be coming to terms with his wife's infidelity. The man who held up the checkout line, using a dozen coupons, may have been laid off from his job of twenty-five years. The neighbor who thinks your children make too much noise may have been diagnosed with terminal cancer. And likewise, these individuals may not recognize your struggle.

While all people will undergo some degree of tragedy in their lives, their accounts won't render themselves the same. Individual trauma manifests as isolated experiences. The hurt that is shared by many will go unseen. It is up to us to emanate compassion. The world needs us to trust and care for one another.

Set boundaries. Sustain yourself with a supportive routine, prioritizing rest periods. Take the space you require, releasing the guilt of explaining yourself to others. Determine what preserves your spirit: supportive employment, bodywork, mental health services, etc., and seek out what your soul needs.

Explore the resistance. When your mind corners you into fear, anxiety, or trepidation, see these as signals that you are ready to grow and evolve. Breathe through your triggers and tiptoe toward extending your self-awareness.

For instance, on a sorrowful anniversary, is it possible to honor yourself (or a loved one that has passed) with acts of love? Profound transformation is available to you, if only you muster the strength to explore these opportunities.

Release your expectations. You can't *move past this* trauma, or *move from this* trauma, or *move through this* trauma. This isn't a life stage that can be fast-forwarded or conquered. The action that needs to occur isn't *movement from something*; it's **opening to everything**. Opening up is the counteraction to closing yourself off.

Let go of what you *think* your future will be. You will still hold space for what was lost – this will not be forgotten. But you owe it to yourself, your family, and your heartbreak to open to the abundance that surrounds you. In the case of a passing loved one, what would they want for you?

Unleash your emotions. Share your sorrow. Find safe expanses to dispense your grief: a good friend, a talk therapist, a journal, a canvas, or a room full of strangers (as you're on stage, armed with a guitar). Look for those who will listen instead of jumping in to offer advice. Run a few miles or hit a punching bag. The sweat and tears may fall simultaneously; let them flow. Express yourself fully and completely.

Find the stillness of the present moment. Be with the pain. Witness what is real to you. Name it. Acknowledge it instead of burying it or pushing it aside. In times of distress, remain present. Recognize that you can hold and honor this space while still actively experiencing the world around you.

Serve the world. Offer assistance to groups or individuals who are suffering in some way. By easing the burden of another, it may help to abate the hurt you carry within you. You can engage in charitable work, volunteering, or social services. Through these inspirational activities, you'll encounter instances of inner peace through introspection and reflection.

Look for a star. The star is the symbol of healing, protection, and spiritual guidance. It reminds us that we are being cared for. In those painful moments of desperation and desolation, look for a star. The star may appear as a twinkle in the eye of a loved one, as a beacon illuminating the night sky, or even ubiquitously as a quality marker on an online review. Welcome the star's serene energy; open your heart to this loving sign and let it wash over you.

Healing will require you to withstand the ultimate act of bravery: faith in yourself. Resources surround you – never feel alone. No matter how bleak the world may seem, through your will and your warmth, there is always hope. And if you look for it, you will find it.

Our deepest wounds reveal our greatest strengths.

You are loved, even if you don't feel that way. Remember those who believe in you. Never forget: You are safe. You are precious. Your inner strength is surging through you.

EXPLORE YOUR SOUL PURPOSE

Have you ever been entirely consumed by a task at hand? Jess paints detailed portraits onto her friend's fingernails. Hiresh meticulously decorates cookies for his daughter's bake sale. And Annie plans her vacation itineraries down to the minute. These are examples of individuals who have been naturally engrossed by a singular activity.

If you find yourself mindlessly working far past the goal at hand or hypnotically losing track of time, survey the situation by asking: **Am I soulfully engaged, or am I out of touch?**

It is vital to question your actions, or else you'll never determine if you're spending your valuable time in a wholesome way. By following your trail of personal curiosities and pondering them deeply, you'll determine what captures your interest and inspires your imagination, which may lead you to your purpose in life.

There is only one of you! And you're here, on this Earth, to make the most of your purpose. The world depends on its impassioned occupants.

Your purpose is your reason for being. Start to determine your purpose by identifying *what you want* and *why you want it* (sometimes, firming up *what you don't want* will highlight *what you do*!). Once you know this, you can start to lean toward your purpose.

Your soul purpose is your commitment to an energetic exchange with the world. Whether art, advocacy, commerce, wellness, etc., your purpose reflects what intrinsically motivates you, expresses your spirit in physical form, and establishes how you choose to serve the world and contribute to the lives of others. And, let's be honest, the actions that serve as clues to your purpose, no matter how big or small those actions may seem, probably feel so *easy* to you that you may be overlooking or dismissing their significance.

Maybe the previous examples highlight individuals whose purposes are as follows: Jess feels called to help others feel beautiful. Hiresh shows others how to nourish all five senses through food. And Annie helps others regard travel as a life-changing experience.

Clarifying your purpose takes conscious consideration. It's one thing to know your purpose, but it's another to act on it. Life may still ask you to keep your day job, heal from medical matters, or even foster children who need a loving home – and yes, those things **need** your attention, but don't lose sight of your purpose. Discover ways to live through your purpose in almost everything you do. Your purpose will inspire you, help you to thrive in conjunction with daily demands, and fill your spiritual cup.

When ready, articulate your purpose clearly within groups you can trust. A well-informed purpose can guide your decisions, influence your behavior, and hint at future goals. You'll be able to seize those moments that light you up when the opportunities arise. Eventually, you'll actualize your purpose in multiple ways with eager abandon.

Make your soul purpose your sole purpose. And the Earth? Well, it will smile upon you.

MAKING MAGIC

Magic is a straightforward concept. It is the ability to wield unseen forces to influence the world around us. But magic takes one essential secret ingredient: belief.

Belief creates feelings that create thoughts, which cause attraction. Know yourself first, determine what you want, then ... become a magnet. You'll start to draw in all that serves you and repel what does not.

Belief is the most commanding incantation there is. What you give power has power. Because of belief's relationship with thought, it is said that if you alter your thoughts, you'll transform your life.

Activate the magic from your very fingertips using your personal power to release the boundless energy within you. When you consciously affirm what you want, the universe will conspire with you. You mold the material world with your thoughts.

Beware! Because toxic thoughts will deflate your spirit and eclipse your worldview. By exposing assumptions, presumptions, and generalizations, you can sharpen your focus toward what you wholeheartedly wish to see. Muster your mettle. You'll find that even the slightest shift toward the light can strip your darkest fears of their strength.

Culture wants us to push, achieve, and stay constantly active. But life doesn't work that way. In fact, nature goes dormant because fallow periods prepare soil for planting, where growth can occur.

You may have to wait. You may have to be still. Magic promises no timeframe.

But the potential is yours. You decide when to think and when not to think. You choose when to assess, when to act, and when to rest. There is always a gap between announcing and obtaining your desire, and the distance you must traverse is determined by one thing: belief. Be bold with your magic.

When one finally takes leadership over the thoughts in their heads, well, they've mastered magic. Because the undeniable fact is: **Whatever you believe, you become.**

AN INTENTIONAL, HEARTFELT HEAD START

Every moment is an opportunity to reinvent yourself. You don't have to wait for the first break of daylight, the first of the month, or the first of the year. With motive and reason as your sidekicks, you can institute a fresh start whenever you damn well please. Whether it's a new direction or a renewed ambition, setting a heartfelt intention can direct your attention.

Intentions are flexible, feeling-based declarations set in the here and now. Goals, on the other hand, are static, achievement-based objectives and typically set for the future.

Examples of intentions include:

- I intend to be my most authentic self.
- I choose to connect deeply with my family.
- I suspend judgment and communicate kindness.

- I feel uplifted when I fully open my heart.
- I follow through and keep my promises.
- I mindfully consume and nourish myself.

When you set an intention, it encourages you to feel the impact of your personal choices. Intentions are proactive and decisive. They are realistic and attainable.

Establish a personal intention by following the steps below:

1. **Meditate.** Find some quiet space to clarify how you want to feel, omitting adverse thinking, self-sabotage, or outdated beliefs.
2. **Create a memorable, positive, present-tense statement.** Take time to select your words thoughtfully. Write them down. Read them aloud. Feel them in your soul.
3. **Invite your words to inspire you.** Repeatedly expose yourself to the phrase – write it on sticky notes, create an image as your cell phone's wallpaper, and repeat it to yourself every time you put on your shoes. Presently and utterly accept the mindset you've visualized.
4. **Check in with yourself to remain accountable.** Before you sleep each night, review your day and look for examples of your intention in action. Adjust your intention as you see fit. If your intention has served you, thank it and honor it.

A thoughtful intention can reframe your mindset in the moment, shifting you into spiritual alignment. Intentions aren't about shooting for the stars; they're about settling into the brightness of your being.

CLEAR OUT THE CLUTTER

There is a direct correlation: If you have a cluttered house, you have a cluttered mind.

In a cluttered environment – home or mind – the energy can't move, becoming stagnant.

Sarah once had a cluttered home. Clothing piled in her bedroom, bills and random papers coated her tabletops, rarely-moved furniture left deep indentations on the carpeting, and bits and bobs from half-completed maintenance projects covered every surface in her basement.

So, for 21 days, Sarah cleaned.

On Day 1, she decided to start in the bedroom, picked an untidy corner, and took ten minutes to organize it. With each item, Sarah decided whether to pitch it, donate it, or use it. For those items that she just wasn't sure about, she'd leave them there.

On Day 2, she started in the same corner again, addressing the items she had been unsure about the day before: older birthday cards, unread dusty books, comfy sweatpants covered in holes. She would hold the item and say, "Does this offer me value anymore?" Knowing when something has served us and is ready to be released is a spiritual blessing.

On Day 3, Sarah addressed the same corner again until it was finally clean.

On Day 4, she knew she wanted to start a new corner, but she first returned to the old one and assessed its condition. She picked up a jacket from yesterday, folded a blanket from this morning, and then moved on to the new corner, implementing her pitch/donate/use system. Days 5, 6, and 7 saw the same system repeated.

On Day 8, Sarah revisited the first corner, as she'd done each day, and added the second corner to this routine to ensure everything was staying organized. Then she pushed forward with her plan and focused on a new area.

After 21 days, and to her great surprise, she had three spotless rooms and established momentum to continue this process throughout her entire house.

Now Sarah feels more settled, clear, and peaceful on the inside, reflecting her environment around her, as if she had dusted the cobwebs from her mind *and* the basement. Both her inner and outer landscapes are beginning to align. Sarah even finds herself giving proper thought to anything she purchases now! It will take only a quick walkthrough in the future to ensure that her home is tidy.

An example of her intention might be: **When I strip away the excess, simple joys can be savored.**

So often, we don't know where to start. But committing ourselves to small tasks over time can collectively create big accomplishments. This works for to-do lists, exercise programs, or any projects one's working on! Break down the behemoth into smaller tasks and beat that failure mentality.

DISCOVER YOUR SELF *Recap*

- *Bodily sensations can be clues to spiritual shifts.*
- *Triggers disconnect you from the present moment. Remember that you are safe and not experiencing the same trauma.*
- *Healing is the processing of painful life experiences and extending yourself permission to emerge renewed.*
- *Your soul purpose is your commitment to an energetic exchange with the world.*
- *Belief is the most commanding incantation there is. What you give power has power.*
- *A thoughtful intention can reframe your mindset in the moment, shifting you into spiritual alignment.*
- *Committing ourselves to small tasks over time can collectively create big accomplishments.*

Three

MANIFEST YOUR DESIRES

Do ideas frequently "pop" into your head without rhyme or reason? These bolts of inspiration may seem nonsensical, but you know, without a doubt, that you are exhilarated. You are transported back to your childhood when you dreamed of the life you would create before anyone tainted your spirit with all the reasons it would surely not come to pass. Now, it's time to stop imagining the worst and start activating the best.

FEELINGS GUIDE LIFE DESIGN

Why have we become so complacent with our one and only lives? Why do we acquiesce to forfeiting our hopes and desires? Why are we okay with letting ourselves down?

It is your birthright to live your life to the fullest.

Now is the time to claim authority over your destiny. Decide how you want to feel – emotionally, physically, spiritually – and then, *and only then*, determine what actions to take to express those feelings.

For instance, if you wish to *feel* untethered, a life without children may be your preference. On the other hand, you may opt to be the head of a large family if you yearn to *feel* maternal.

If you want to *feel* quietude, a celebrity life might seem suffocating. However, you may embrace the starring role at the local theatre if your genuine desire is to *feel* seen.

It takes honest inquiry to live your best life and discernment to select passions that reflect your unique self and soul. This work is crucial – it's emotionally-informed alchemy at its finest!

The word "feeling" is an abstraction. Ask a dozen people to define this word, and you'll get a dozen answers. But feelings, in this context, are the secret to enjoying your very best life and the essence of your conscious experience. Through great feelings, we harness great power. So, feel everything!

Without allowing yourself to feel, you'd simply go through the motions of life, and what a hollow existence that would be. To sincerely live, you must expose yourself to all of life, allowing yourself to be utterly open, experiencing everything profoundly to the deepest depth of your soul.

Eventually, when you hit the one chord – that ideal feeling – that echoes through your body and into the universe, you'll feel the spark, the light, the vibrancy. You'll marvel at how uplifting and fulfilling your life can be simply because you're *feeling* how you wish to *feel*.

With feelings leading the charge, you'll start to recognize your skills that are currently lying dormant and your perceived "weaknesses" that are, in fact, strengths incognito.

A great way to explore preferred feelings and potential dreams is to consider *what you're already doing* in your downtime. Keenly review your recent web browser history, the email alerts you have read, your watch lists on streaming services, and the individuals you follow on social media. Think about the things you doodle, the activities in which you lose yourself, the person whose calls you never miss, and the cities you love to frequent. Which of these bits of information evoke the *feelings* you wish to *feel?*

Whatever it is, dive into it. Investigate these cosmic clues by assembling a vision board, free-writing, meditating, or chatting with a good friend. **Envision the life that *feels* best to you.**

GOAL-DEN OPPORTUNITIES

Why *can't* you have *everything* you want?

You can. You most certainly can! And you don't have to settle for anything less. By knowing how you want to feel, you'll be able to know what you want, which will help you determine where you need to go.

If you could have anything in life, what would it be?

Write yourself a letter, in the present tense, of what you want your future to look like in two to three years, taking into consideration relationships, career, wealth, spirituality, health, community, and whatever other details you deem important. The bigger the dream, the better.

For example:

>*Dear Me,*
>
>*I am alive! I wake up each morning in my Bar Harbor bungalow. The shimmering lake reflects the sunshine. The cool breezes refresh me. I'm smiling through the shivers. The publishing advance for my fifth book was just confirmed at $150,000. I can't wait to get started ... but first, a handful of blueberries, plucked straight from my backyard!*
>
>*My husband and I will be hiking through Acadia National Forest this afternoon, with our old dog leading the way. She knows the trails better than we do!*
>
>*Love always,*
>
>*Myself*

Imagine yourself living and breathing this scenario. How might you feel at your very core? Name those feelings and invoke them *now*.

Feeling aspirational feelings *now* will help guide us toward intentionally creating the life we wish to design. After penning your wishful thinking, say "thank you," as if it's already happened. Then you can start whimsically planning by clarifying your goals and up-grading them into action plans.

A gentle note: There is no need to put undue pressure on yourself. Sometimes it's a much more sustainable, richer experience if we tiptoe across the steppingstones instead of diving straight into the deep end. So be mindful of your intensity.

For instance, if Doug is considering quitting his job, we're not advocating for him to spray paint his resignation on the side of his office building. We're simply suggesting that Doug take exploratory actions: Doug can polish his résumé, register on a few job search websites, and ping his network for opportunities that fit his ideal profession.

All this to say, instead of taking a wayward plunge, it's fine to test the water temperature first. Dip your feet in, lean back, and think, "Why can't I ...?"

The glaring reality is: There's no reason you can't. Every inch toward a goal is a reason to revel, so keep moving in the direction that feels most aligned and know that you always control the momentum.

EVERY ACT IS AN ACT OF CREATION

You are the designer of your life; therefore, any action you take, whether blatantly participating or passively observing, is an act of creation. From routinely brushing your teeth to courageously leading your choir for the first time, every task (mundane or sensational) carries energy and informs the next.

It's quite simple. You raise and lower your vibrations systematically. Engaging in digressive chatter, purchasing way more than you need, eating chemically processed foods, and like activities will lower your frequency. Conversely, donating your time, complimenting others, displaying empathy, and similar actions will raise your frequency.

Every moment of every day, you are laying the foundations for future growth and expansion. Getting in touch with your feelings will help you become intentional with your time, focus, and energy.

Now comes the work. As 21st-century mortal beings, we exist in a material society with a capitalist economy and cultural rules. We can't ignore the "real world."

However, achievement without purpose makes for hollow success, evidenced by unwanted emotions, such as ungratefulness, bitterness, and disappointment.

So, push yourself past rote explanations, ordinary expectations, and perceived "norms." Invite big ideas to rouse your soul. Let daily challenges add richness to your adventure. Follow your heart, not the rules, because you decide where your energy flows. Behold your soul's ripple effect as it transforms the world around you.

FAILING FORWARD

So, we've all been there: we bombed a job interview, we didn't make the cut at tryouts, we lost a big client, we overpromised our time, we let a secret slip, we missed a deadline. We failed.

You're embarrassed, discouraged, frustrated. You shield your eyes and whisper, "Ugh. My life is over."

What do you do?

Absorb it. That's right. Absorb it.

Absorb this experience as a testament to the condition of being human. It happened. Life is messy. You can't have good times all the time, and the hard times will pass, too.

Take a moment or (many, many) more to grieve. Cry. It. Out. Apologize (if necessary). Then inch yourself toward self-acceptance. The sting may not feel any less severe right now, but the pain will diminish with time.

Was the mistake as detrimental as you are making it to be? Failures can range from inconvenient to colossal, yet chances are the ramifications of this fallout are survivable. This hiccup will be old news quickly; absorb the anguish by projecting a mental image of how you'll feel two weeks from now.

Processing defeat (whether publicly, privately, or both) takes time, compassion, and finesse; you can't shortcut the proceeding. Handle each situation on an individual basis. Pause and ask yourself: **What's truly bothering me?**

Just because you failed doesn't mean you're a failure.

We often view ourselves through what we do. But it's time to consider ourselves for who we are.

Eventually, the lessons will emerge. Turn your setbacks into set-ups with self-inquiry. If you ...

- **Bombed the interview**: Was this job the best fit in the first place? What is your method for interview prep?
- **Didn't make the cut**: Is this something you truly want? Will you make an effort in earnest to improve?
- **Lost a big client:** How can you learn from this experience to bolster your existing relationships?
- **Overpromised your time:** How can you define and articulate your boundaries better?
- **Let a secret slip:** Did you share this information by mistake, or decide to reveal what you knew? Why?
- **Missed a deadline:** Can you use your powerful "no" to prioritize the things that matter?

So, will you give up? Or will you make a comeback?

There may be valid reasons for both. And it's not the choice itself that matters. The reason for your choice is what defines your true character.

Fearing failure is worse than failure itself.

In the end, if you're *failing*, you're *doing something*. You're taking chances. You're pushing yourself. You're putting your wants and needs on the line. You are both lionhearted *and* vulnerable. And, brave soul, that takes one hell of a lot of gumption.

So, let obstacles make you nimble and difficulties make you stronger. Grow through the pain. May this failure be the force that launches you forward and hoists you to rise to the next challenge.

SOULFUL SELF-CARE

Self-care is often thought of as mini-vacations, facial masks, and chocolate bars. And unquestionably, these things are *gifts we give ourselves out of love.* However, it is essential to transcend surface offerings and tend deeply to our souls for lasting well-being.

Let us be clear: There is *no* shame in intentional self-care in all its forms and fashions. Self-care is a relative notion and might change daily, self-expression being a visual mode of self-care. But soulful self-care – *true, authentic, Higher Self self-care* – requires reflection and answering the question: **How can I best nourish myself?**

Soulful self-care can sometimes feel like tough love. It's a heaping dose of essential medicine; overall, beneficial for your health, but it can taste a little bitter at first.

It can manifest as either small or large choices (often *hard choices*) that sustain your long-term wellness: a fulfilling conversation instead of a scroll session on social media, a bottle of water instead of a carafe of wine, an unscheduled midday work break instead of answering another five emails.

Soulful self-care is telling yourself what you *need* to hear instead of what you *want* to hear.

When we are clear on our true desires, self-care can reinforce firm boundaries that we've established for our personal betterment.

Self-care is not to be relegated as a luxury you accept each time you have a few extra minutes or dollars to spare. Self-care is your right, your responsibility to the one and only entity that is you. And thus, self-care must be actively asserted daily with unquestionable tenacity.

Take very good care of yourself, my friend, and don't you dare apologize for it.

HARNESSING YOUR CRAFT

Just like the body and mind, the spirit must be exercised regularly to operate optimally. When we neglect our spiritual development, we feel energetically stagnant, psychically foggy, and metaphysically impoverished.

Many fully-immersive, magically-oriented undertakings can be employed for soulful alignment and intuitive prowess. But there's no standardized approach to any of them, so you should try your hand at a variety of options before determining which ones enhance your awareness.

The bottom line is that committing wholeheartedly to any practice can be a form of active meditation. So try not to overthink during your exploration stage and just let go. You'll know when you've identified the right fit. The entire ethereal cosmos within you is clamoring to be unleashed.

Below are some engaging, expansive ways to raise your vibrations and channel your psychic abilities:

- **Free-write:** Your Higher Source leaps from your pen when you vanquish your inner editor.
- **Practice Yoga:** Balance, breathwork, and flexibility are the big takeaways.
- **Play music:** Strum away and connect with ancestors by executing the same chords played centuries ago.
- **Get moving:** Dance, run, and push your muscles. Completely lose yourself in the moment.
- **Consult tarot, runes, etc.:** Visual cues can reframe our perspectives and our preconceived notions.
- **Create something:** Draw, scrapbook, paint. Your intuition provides a wellspring of ideas. Also, bonus points if you sculpt while being blindfolded.
- **Interpret your dreams:** While sleeping, the subconscious mind emanates through your intuitive faculties.
- **Meditate:** A period of quiet reflection will help funnel messages from your Higher Source.
- **Engage in stichomancy:** Grab a book off the shelf, flip to a page, and point to a paragraph. Reflect on the very first words you read.
- **Spend time in nature:** Go analog for a day and see what bubbles up from the brook inside you.

Getting started is up to you. Classes, how-to books, and instructional videos are plentiful and will teach you the basics through the esoteric. But at the end of the day, doing something "correctly" is far less important than feeling invigorated by the activity.

Be with your body, observe your boundaries, and show up as often as you feel called to do.

Your participation and sincere desire will tap into the collective unconscious. And with each session, you'll unearth hidden aspects of your awareness and sense a slight edge in life. With your insight on the uptick, you'll perceive your own unique personal evolution.

Practice doesn't make perfect. Practice upgrades us.

These practices are incredibly beneficial in moments of doubt, upheaval, resistance, inertia, etc. Tools can operate as a conduit for your energy. They can anchor you to the present moment by highlighting struggles, transcending tedious irritations, processing emotional pain, and ultimately enhancing self-awareness. By working with your chosen tools, you can trust yourself to quash lingering self-doubt and summon enormous reserves of self-belief.

RALLY YOUR SOUL SQUAD

When you start actualizing a goal, there comes a time when you notice the buzz of excitement, and you sense your energy expanding. At this point, it is time to assemble your support team.

Consider the "Day Dreamers," the "Go-Getters," the intrepid ones who encourage your reveries, no matter how silly your musings may seem.

By connecting with people and institutions that stand behind you, you'll begin to witness your own follow-through. Momentum will build. They will help move your projects forward with action, strategy, and focus. Steps will seem less nebulous. Suddenly, you know what you need to research. You know who you need to call. You know what task you need to do.

When you freely share yourself with like-minded souls and kindred spirits, you receive the community they offer in return. This encouragement revitalizes your efforts and endeavors. You'll feel into potentialities you never thought possible. When you trust your vision and believe in yourself, doors will open, and you'll be welcomed into places you never envisioned you'd go.

ABOVE ALL ELSE, KEEP GOING

When you show your true strength, you conquer that which hinders you from experiencing love. And oftentimes, the things that stand in your way are the very same ones you have the privilege of doing: folding the laundry, washing the dishes, scrubbing the floors, repainting the shed, etc.

You can do anything, but you can't do everything.

Everything may seem important, but not everything is of great urgency. It's time to assert the mindset that you always maintain the ability to choose what you prioritize, reschedule, or eliminate altogether. And if you feel overwhelmed or just in need of respite, pitch the to-do list and bring your desires front and center by creating a non-negotiables list.

For example, Tory aims to connect more with her sister, so perhaps her list might look something like this: "To cherish my sister, for the next month, I will peruse that old box of childhood photos, refuse to think unkindly of her, call her once a week just to check in on her family, and envision a reason I am grateful for her each night."

Our non-negotiables list reminds us of what we've established as most important. Tory may find that with intentional focus, she will begin to conjure feelings of love for her sister organically throughout daily life.

As we grow and expand, so do our priorities. However, with careful discernment, we can assert a focus area that is paramount to all others.

Life will ebb and flow, for that is the nature of all things. Standing up for yourself and your intentions can be difficult, but it is the foremost method of avoiding regret. It is a verifiable fact that that which pulls at your heartstrings is meant to be part of your journey, even if you're not the *best* at it.

How many times were dreams shattered because we bowed out just a moment too soon?

Be aware of the occasions when you procrastinate; it's a coping mechanism that may stem from being paralyzed by perfection. However, perfection is a fantasy, and the counteraction to perfection is completion. Finish this stage, watch yourself grow, and realize that authenticity outweighs perfection every time.

And if the rules don't suit you, break them. Let your morals be high, and trust yourself to go your own way. You'll never have anything to show of your love if you always talk yourself out of taking a step forward. So, go onward, my friend, no matter the distance.

MANIFEST YOUR DESIRES *Recap*

- *Assert your desires by starting with how you want to feel.*
- *It's okay to dream big and then inch forward.*
- *Every act is an act of creation, so act with intent.*
- *Failure doesn't mean the end. Turn your setbacks into setups with self-inquiry.*
- *Self-care nourishes you best with focused action.*
- *Magic fills your space and soul when you engage in activities that both develop and refine your intuitive capabilities.*
- *Your soul squad of go-getters can help you actualize your dreams.*
- *It is a verifiable fact that that which pulls at your heartstrings is meant to be part of your journey, even if you're not the "best" at it.*

Four

LOVE YOUR LIFE

The beauty outside of you reflects the beauty within. Suspending judgment and extending forgiveness paves the way to radical, unbridled freedom, so offer yourself nothing short of unconditional love.

BE YOUR BIGGEST FAN

It's easy to be your own harshest critic, your worst enemy, especially when no one else seems to be clapping for you. However, prolonged bouts of *tough love* can obliterate your self-esteem and your self-worth. By not extending yourself grace, you prevent opportunities that would otherwise flow easily to you.

So, we propose a different path: What if, instead, you were fanatical about yourself? What if you accepted yourself – wholly and completely – for one day? Not one foul word. Not one disapproval. Not one unkind remark. Only offerings of support and encouragement.

How would this feel in your body and mind? How might you radiate this feeling outward?

There is a spirit that burns within you. So fan your fire.

Be excessive in your adoration. Let the air of encouragement brighten your spark. Let your motivation be your tinder. Let your positivity be your kindling. Let your commitment be your firewood. Stoke, don't smother. And then pause and bask in the warmth of your innate brilliance.

PAUSE YOUR JUDGMENT

When we judge another, we are forming an instinctive opinion about them, usually based on little evidence. This comparison is toxic because we are essentially separating ourselves from others, further displacing the serenity of connectivity.

For instance, Liz works with a cantankerous man named Eddie, who often pollutes their work environment with his skeptical, grouchy attitude. Whenever Eddie's behavior irks Liz, she imagines Eddie as a close relation that she loves (i.e., her father). When Liz views Eddie through the lens of love, she releases the tension that she holds and finds more space for understanding.

Judgment is a defense mechanism that stems from unwanted emotions: envy, jealousy, anger, irritation, etc. It is far better to enjoy the feeling of well-being for another. Project love. Project kindness. Project happiness. Acknowledge their existence and their desire for the life they visualize. Imagine your heart center comingling with theirs. Then settle into the growth of gratitude in your being.

A kind note: If you feel perpetually exposed to and provoked by flagrant comparison, you may just need a break. Identify the source, and then silence the news feed, the group text, and the photo reel for whatever time period you deem appropriate. Tell only those you choose. A firm boundary can be your biggest ally.

But above all else, stay attuned to those around you who may be displacing their own insecurities. Your job may be the desire of someone seeking purpose. Your relationship may be the desire of someone seeking companionship. Your home may be the desire of someone seeking shelter.

Be mindful of your blessings and bounty and, come what may, exude deep appreciation and awareness. Don't lose sight of the abundance surrounding you.

TREASURE YOUR VESSEL

Your body, your life's external container, is simply marvelous! The holder of your bones, muscles, and organs works tirelessly on your behalf so you can do your good work throughout the world. It is the vessel through which you breathe, move, digest, think, and feel.

Mindful respect for your body replaces shame and judgment with love and appreciation, opening one up to unparalleled spiritual growth. Here are some ways to offer care and compassion for the one and only you:

- **Get moving:** Even a brisk 20-minute walk will leave you happier and healthier. When your blood flows, creative energy naturally increases.

- **Eat mindfully:** Consume a balanced, clean, nutrient-rich diet of colorful foods. Once you fuel your body, what will you do with this energy?
- **Ditch the poisons:** Over-consumption of alcohol, cigarettes, and caffeine interferes with mental clarity and distracts us from the natural wonders of the world.
- **Hydrate heavily:** Drinking plenty of water flushes away harmful toxins. Consume slowly, methodically, and constantly.
- **Get your ZZZs:** Restful periods of sleep serve as powerful restoratives for our minds and bodies so that they may operate at their optimal levels.

Your body is an incredible biological machine and a miracle to behold. Choose to cherish your physical self every day in every way.

COURAGEOUS FORGIVENESS

You've undoubtedly heard the adage "Forgive and forget." However, we believe, "Forgive and be free."

You are, no matter what, capable of forgiveness.

That may come across as a bold statement, but it's true. Forgiveness is a self-concept that exists *only within you.*

Forgiveness is difficult but crucial for peace of mind. It is a conscious choice to release feelings of resentment, vengeance, and indignation. These feelings can be directed toward someone who has harmed you or someone who has harmed another.

During those times when you actively stop yourself from forgiving, you are clenching hurt that only affects *you*. It's akin to drinking poison and expecting the other person to suffer the effects.

One way to work through forgiveness is to surrender the pain by penning a letter:

1. **Construct:** Write a letter to the person (living or passed) who has hurt, disappointed, and/or abused you. Tell them your experience of their wrongdoing, how they made you feel, the lessons you learned, and how you will effectively serve the world now as a more enlightened person.
2. **Release:** Once finished, visualize sending them soft light and disengage with them. Do not reread the letter. By writing, you're releasing; should you reread, you are inviting yourself to take it all back in.
3. **Finalize:** Do not mail this letter. Do not keep it. Burn or shred the page, and then feel its negative vibrations loosen, effectively dissolving the bars that have imprisoned you.
4. **Process:** You never have to share this experience with another soul. This is your personal journey, and your growth and development are never determined by another's perception.

A word of advice: Begin slowly and methodically. Don't automatically jump to the person who triggers you the most. You'll know when the time for forgiveness is right, so perhaps don't attempt to start with forgiving your abusive, alcoholic uncle; begin with your coworker who was outwardly rude in the office the other day.

If you don't learn how to fully forgive someone, you ultimately fuse yourself to that person through hate, anger, bitterness, disgust, and resentment. By *not* forgiving, you are deciding not to move forward. You are, in essence, trying to find solace in guilt and sadness, which you are mistakenly perceiving as some semblance of control in the situation. However, it's the other person who is controlling you. You are stuck in that tender, unjust moment and not working through it, so it will energetically reside in your body, blocking space where greatness could be.

To forgive someone requires your acceptance, not theirs.

Whether or not someone deserves your forgiveness is beside the point. A focused subject is a component of forgiveness, but the subject's participation is not necessary. You don't need to commune with someone to forgive them.

Forgiveness is not to be confused with pardon, mercy, or leniency. Forgiveness does not tolerate another's behavior; it does not excuse their choices. When you forgive someone, you're not saying, "What you did to me is okay." You're saying, "What you did will no longer be judged by me." Their fate is now between them and their Higher Power.

When we forgive someone, we may have to accept a current reality that we wish had not come to pass and our role in the circumstance. Forgiveness is a deliberate decision to embrace the present moment by accepting the past. Sometimes, the hardest person to forgive is ourselves.

Here are the straightforward facts: We make our own happiness. We make our own closure. We make our own forgiveness. The power is solely yours; don't let another person take away your power. Only you determine your soul's freedom; no one else.

REAL BEAUTY IS ENERGY

True, genuine beauty is based on energetic *presence* rather than physical *appearance*. Beauty starts from within, beginning with the lifestyle you lead. Our outsides reflect our insides, which go way beyond skin deep.

Remember, mirrors are portals. As you speak to yourself in your reflection, you speak straight through to your soul.

You don't have to maintain a certain body type, follow current trends, spend a lot of money, or hide your *professed* imperfections to feel and extend your best. Here are some guaranteed ways to conjure natural beauty:

- **Express your soul:** Smile, *but only if it feels right*. Relax, drop your guard, and invite softness into your space.
- **Be yourself:** Be goofy. Be silly. Be genuine. Don't give a hoot what others think. Embrace non-conformity. Have a sense of humor.
- **Savor the moment:** Sip slowly. Linger longer. Laugh loudly. Play harder. Lose yourself in that which enriches your soul. And don't fall victim to mindless texting, scrolling, or complaining.
- **Be decisive:** Make the first move. Know what you want. Say what you want. Pursue what you want.

- **Connect deeply:** Have intense conversations. Listen (bonus points for looking another in the eye!). And then hold another's secrets tightly.
- **Be warmhearted:** Approach life with optimism and stability. Let your maternal/paternal instincts kick in. Give credit where it is due. Help out. Get along with people.
- **Own your style:** It doesn't matter how you dress. Let your soul soar and it will visually represent you!
- **Walk with confidence:** Assert yourself while you amble and never *ever* be afraid to take up space.

Patience, kindness, attention – that's pure beauty. And on every level, the beauty you choose to see reflects the beauty within you.

YOUR *KEYED-UP* COMPANION: THE EGO

When you ask, "Who am I?" you will likely respond with beliefs about yourself. This forms your sense of identity, your self-concept, or your ego.

Your ego is what you choose to believe about yourself and how you see yourself within the world. And your ego likes to keep things steady. It wants to keep you safe: "No, no. Don't go over *there* because look what we have *here*. If you *do* go over there, I don't know what I can do for you." The ego tries to act like our best friend but is tainted by our thoughts and fears.

For instance, true relationships will always have a little tension, and sometimes your spouse says something you deem out of line. Your response reflects your ego. When you are in your light, you send your spouse love and continue doing what you're doing, unaffected by the comment. When you are in a state of lower vibrations, you may feel defensive and snap back with, "How dare you say that to me?"

Chris was passed over for a promotion at work. He could construe the decision as, "My boss is a jerk! His decision is ludicrous. He just doesn't like me. The person they promoted is incompetent!" That's his ego.

You can either blame others or step back and learn.

Chris may alternatively process the situation as, "How can I be more prepared for opportunities?" or "Maybe this is the best because there is a better fit for me elsewhere."

Your ego is hesitant to grow because growth brings change and discomfort, and your ego doesn't want you to step outside of your comfort zone. Your ego limits your ability to connect with people and thus lowers your vibrations. It closes you off from the world. It *wants* you to stay precisely as it *wants* you to think you are.

But the beauty of your ego is that it will always go with you. It loves you. It needs you. It never leaves your side. So, if you rise, it will rise with you. Foster your ability to question your internal monologue, challenge your ego, and regularly reevaluate your beliefs.

Your ego will always try to stop you from taking a leap because it's much safer to take a few steps back from the edge of that cliff. But if you will yourself to bound into the canyon with your bungee gear, because you *just know* it's in your best interest to jump, you'll find your ego tethered to your side, likely sporting a selfie stick.

LOVING THROUGH EXASPERATION

"Well, thankfully, your cousins don't seem to be plagued by the many problems that have befallen you ..."

Thanks, Aunt Effie. Thanks for your take on things.

Are you finding it hard to relate to your relatives?

We've all been there. Someone you *really, really want to* love is driving you **mad**. With 7.7 billion unique personalities on Earth, there's bound to be a little tension. And some of us are most challenged by those with whom we share close social proximity: controlling family members, nagging coworkers, nosy neighbors, etc., which leave us angry, irritated, and annoyed.

There are no accidents. These situations are gifts. Triggers are signs of what we need to work through and release to find peace and serenity in our hearts.

How can we ensure feelings aren't hurt and make the most out of one another's company? Well, creating a tender (and fulfilling!) middle ground is not only possible but can be pleasurable.

Temper your emotional weather: What's going on with you? Look inward to see if you've simply had a bad day. You may be transposing your funkiness and impatience on a loved one (e.g., throwing emotional spears at an easy target).

For example, if you've been stressing over money and a child excitedly asks you to play, you may flip out and scream, "I don't have time!" Stop for a second. Review what thoughts you had right before your blowout. Perspective and clarification may allow you to recalibrate, neutralize, and apologize.

Communicate deliberately: Connect thoroughly and stay present. When sharing your feelings, pause to ask yourself first, "Is this true?" If so, speak! But be prudent with gossip, conflict, and sweeping generalizations. Show consideration by choosing the appropriate time and place to take a stand. Check yourself before righteousness surprises you with an unwelcome appearance.

Find empathy: It's therapeutic to approach others with understanding, appreciation, and compassion. Recognize, through all their faults, foibles, and follies, that they're only human. They're not out to hurt you. They're just doing their very best for themselves and their families and trying to survive in this crazy yet beautiful world – *just like you*. Humanity is a humbling equalizer.

Bolster your inner fortitude: In extreme moments of trial, it takes focus and effort to extend love to others. Be cognizant of when to connect and when to walk away. Sometimes the situation requires you to swallow the "last word" and shut down a topic by gracefully excusing yourself to the restroom.

And the next time Aunt Effie calls, don't automatically pick up the phone. Take a moment to breathe and assess your current emotional temperament by asking, "Am I in the right state of mind to chat?" If you decide to converse, set an intention before you commune, such as, "My soul enjoys brief, pleasant conversation."

You can't expect another to change, and honestly, that's their pre-rogative, not yours. Only within *you* contains the magic for personal evolution.

HONE YOUR HABITS

Every evening, Paige bursts through the door after a long day at work and feels ravenous. Before she even kicks off her heels, she grabs a bar of chocolate. Paige wolfs it down in less than a minute, and then inhales a handful of chips, followed by a slice or two of leftover cheese pizza. She cracks open a can of soda as she scans the cupboard for her next treat. On processed snacks, she buries the stress and malnourishment of the workday.

This is an unhealthy high, a habit Paige knows doesn't serve her. Maybe she's even at the point in her life where she knows what's good for her and what's slowing her down.

Compound habits, over time, whether good or bad, create the future. After a period of time, Paige realizes that she's lacking energy, gaining unhealthy amounts of weight, exhibiting moody behavior in the evenings, and experiencing more cravings. She recognizes the slippery slope.

But why can't Paige change?

She can! And the mere fact that she's taking a precious pause to identify an unhealthy habit is half the battle won.

A habit consists of three components: an impulse, an action, and a reward. Once you acknowledge the stimulus and the compensation, you can modify the behavior. Habits contain neutral, routine actions. It's up to you to determine what actions you will continue to repeat by taking into full account the overall effects of those actions on your life.

To complicate matters, we're creatures of instant gratification. So give yourself a leg up on your habit loop by equipping yourself, eliminating temptations, and prepping in advance.

Going back to the junk food example, let's identify the impulse Paige experiences as a hollow feeling after a stressful day at work, a feeling that is unlikely to change anytime soon. The action is overconsuming something readily available. The reward is that Paige feels more fulfilled.

So, what can Paige do instead? She can enjoy a large, thick protein shake (prepared in advance) as soon as she gets in the door from work. Better yet, while sipping, she can take this time to engage in a brief freewriting exercise on self-inquiry. Same impulse. Same reward. Different action. And now she can distract herself until the habit is reinforced as muscle memory because she's prepared with **something else to do.**

You can't build new routines by simply telling yourself, "Don't eat unhealthy foods." You must engage in a behavior that allows you to enjoy the same reward.

Eventually, Paige may even build momentum to create additional changes. She may insist upon a full half-hour break for a nutritive lunch during her workday, and an evening walk while listening to a personal development podcast.

Practice discernment when you build and reinforce your habits, and those habits will empower you to make consistent, tiny, reflexive choices that will change your life in massive ways.

LOVE YOUR LIFE *Recap*

- *Self-love frees us. Prolonged criticism imprisons us.*
- *Judgment sabotages authentic connection with another.*
- *Your body is marvelous! Treasure it daily.*
- *Forgiveness is the release of trapped emotional associations that do not serve us.*
- *True beauty is an energy, not an appearance.*
- *Your ego is your identity, and through your will, you can mold it to truly represent your beautiful soul.*
- *When loved ones drive you crazy, you've identified a trigger to heal.*
- *Build solid habits to reinforce the foundation of your life.*

Five

HONOR YOUR JOURNEY

Your story is yours alone. With every choice you make and action you take, you fashion an account of your existence. Your story is yours to refine as often as you feel called to do because it is always a work in progress.

ASSERT YOUR STORY

Our life journeys are represented through the stories we craft about ourselves. And in your story, are you the villain, the victim, or the victor? You decide.

Since your birth, millions of messages have been impressed upon you. Some have built you up, and others have broken you down.

This is where your story comes into play. Your story is the culmination of your experiences, memories, and perspectives. Your story explores the continuity of your life, and by recounting events, you ascribe meaning.

Our stories may not read as linear tales, but that's okay because life is spiralic. Only during some time in the future are we able to sense our personal evolution.

So, dig deep to access your seedling of a story. Realize that, at any moment, you can accept yourself as the rare flower you are and choose to grow upward from a place of encouragement, support, and love.

When you start accepting yourself, you create space for yourself and your stories. You give yourself permission to be heard, and then you will speak. You will spiritually evolve from victim to victor.

THE POWER OF PERPETUAL CHANGE

When we hold tight to stories and say, "I'll always be this way." Well … you get what you ask for. Do you feel stuck in the same repeating story, living the same day, over and over again?

You don't have to be a different person to move toward a different outcome. Just approach your story with graceful curiosity. Focus on what you want, not what you don't want. Stand up to the false stories in your mind that keep you in a pattern of awfulizing your worldview.

You alone hold the power to rewrite your past and create your future; therein lies your story. You can accept. You can change. Or you can alter what you know, freeing yourself of so-called pre-determinates.

The next time that you encounter a pervasive, negative thought throughout your day, examine the account your mind has formed:

1. **Identify:** Retell the situation in story form to yourself and include as much detail as you can remember.
2. **Question:** On a sheet of paper, label a column, "**What limiting beliefs am I holding on to?**" Let your response fly from your pen for five minutes.
3. **Consider:** Peruse your list and make a new column labeled, "**What are the possibilities that I'm not seeing?**" And again, for five minutes, let your insight reveal itself alongside your first list.
4. **Reflect:** Notice and honor the shift in your viewpoint. Allow yourself to honor the open-heartedness that poured forth from your Inner Voice.

You're not stuck. Your ego is holding you hostage. To make an upgrade in life, you have to reframe your perspective, get the hell outta your own way, and move forward brandishing the ultimate creative license.

Stories are like outfits; they are the chosen ensemble through which we interact with the world. We wear stories that others respond to. We grow out of stories that feel too juvenile. We expand past stories that are too restrictive. We exude confidence through stories that make us feel good.

So, be mindful of which labels you wear. Tailor your beliefs to suit yourself. Or, more drastically speaking, how about taking it all off and stripping down to your raw, authentic self?

Your story is perpetually evolving, changing, and growing. Release your stories that no longer serve you. What beauty to behold! Being nude never felt so free.

The world is ever-changing, and so are you. You are a different person than you were yesterday. How will you style yourself today?

THE PITFALLS OF PARADIGMS

Paradigms are lies we have bought into, statements that were told to us, or we told them to ourselves. In a scarcity world, we might hear, "Money doesn't grow on trees," "You can't teach an old dog new tricks," "He was born on the wrong side of the tracks," or "Children are meant to be seen and not heard."

Paradigms are messages that have been impressed upon us throughout our lives. These pithy sentences seem harmless enough, but as paradigms, they penetrate our psyches. We then adopt them as accurate models, utterly unaware of their ability to warp our worldviews. When we realize that the "truths" we have heard don't quite sit well with us anymore, we can see them as the lies that they are. But it's up to us to figure this out and make a change.

Claire's a mom of three children, and they live together in a two-bedroom rental. She's been able to tailor her career around her children while making ends meet. Yet, all her extended family continues to say about her is, "Claire knows nothing about money." This paradigm has been impressed upon her for decades.

Yet, somehow, Claire is, in fact, making her life work on a minimal salary. She's putting her children first and running a very successful and happy household.

So, it's not necessarily that Claire knows nothing about money. Claire is convinced she can only *make* so much money, because she believes she only *deserves* so much money, which has capped her salary at $56,300. If Claire feels unfulfilled, it may be because she maintains a scarcity mentality, compounded by the lack-inducing energy continually extended by her relatives. At the end of the day, Claire knows much more about money management than both she and her critics readily recognize.

So often, if you don't dissect what you're being told, you start to believe, "I don't have enough money. Money doesn't come to me. I can't make enough. I struggle with money."

But that's not the case! By shifting our mentalities from scarcity to abundance, we acknowledge all we have brought into our lives with deep gratitude, recognize our inherent value, witness all that is working in our favor, and realize that we are ready to thrive.

When Claire finally tires of the ceiling that she has been cowering under for years, she can throw on her superhero cape, take a step toward advocating her self-worth, and muster the strength to break through all the barriers confining her.

THE WEIGHT OF YOUR WORDS

The English language alone has gifted us 170,000 words and counting. Yet, you probably wish it were possible to return a few.

Because, as the world evolves and awareness expands, we are experiencing the limitations of dated and restrictive language.

The list below features several words that may account for a significant portion of your vocabulary. We invite you to consider releasing these statements and replacing them with options that feel more expansive to you.

Avoid Using	Why?
Could, Would, Should	*Don't feel guilty over paths you didn't take. Trust your journey.*
Right, Wrong	*Our world is not an either/or world.*
Mistake	*Everything is a lesson and a chance to change our patterns.*
Never, Always	*The world doesn't operate in absolutes. See past the perceived "facts" and address the sentiment behind the situation.*
Have to	*Replace with "Get to." Determine what tasks take priority. Find appreciation in daily life.*
Try	*Just do it. Invite yourself to act and be present during the experience.*
If	*Use "when" instead and take ownership of your destiny.*

Release unwanted attachments by carefully curating your language and ensuring your words are lifting you up, instead of knocking you down.

Conversely, some phrases are okay to say, although we may have been taught otherwise.

The following phrases are often attributed as words of weakness, but that's just the societal fear talking. The following list, in fact, features very healthy statements: acts of strength, reflections of deep self-awareness, and promises of self-study.

Your Mouth Says	Your Soul Means
I don't know.	*Let me gather some resources and figure this out.*
I'm sorry.	*This experience has been a learning opportunity. I'll shift my actions and adjust.*
I've changed my mind.	*After exploring the matter, I've opened to another viewpoint or path.*
Why not?	*I imagine possibilities outside of the status quo.*
I need to rethink things.	*I never thought of it that way. I'm interested in your opinion, but I need a moment to let things settle.*

Bring careful awareness to your word choice. Your language evokes emotions, emits verbal vibrations, and brings about a direct response. Take every effort to craft your conversation with intention because *like* attracts *like*, and what you *say* is what you *create*.

MINDFUL COMMUNICATION

The way we choose to communicate influences the tone of our energetic space. All of us have been there: said something we didn't mean and wished we could take back. We insult as a defense mechanism. We exaggerate to get attention. We gossip as a quick way to connect with others. Communication, without tact, harms all parties involved.

To break this cycle, one should practice wholehearted communication. Ask yourself: **Are my words truthful, useful, and intentional?**

Truthful language is simply meaning what you say. You don't lie. You don't exaggerate. This is the truth as you know it and understand it to be.

Useful communication is pointed and helpful. It is well-rounded and enriches our experience. It connects us to one another on a human level.

Intentional word choice ensures you are uber-selective with the vocabulary you use and sensitive to the parties you address. It is a vow to only partake in respectful language.

If the above conditions are not met, pause and take a moment to think before you speak. You may thank yourself later. The more you engage in positive communication, the easier the words will flow in future conversations.

Listening is vital to fully participating in a conversation and deeply developing a relationship. Since we were children, we have been instructed to "Listen closely." And while the sentiment is pure, the directive falls short.

More so than listening, however, *we must pay attention.* This means fully engaging your ears, of course, but also noticing inflection, nonverbal cues, body language, and behavior. Only then are you plugged into the energetic vibrations surrounding you and fully immersed in the conversation. Silence allows for space where we can pour our energy.

When you are offered a compliment, accept it fully and completely. Instead of downplaying praise, take a moment to receive the affection, letting it sink into your heart. Feel the momentum to live out this perspective. Love can be communicated beyond words through attention, actions, and even material items – these languages of love are just as valid.

So, the next time your client bakes you homemade cookies, accept them with a smile and enjoy them thoroughly! Instead of saying, "You really shouldn't have," say, "Thank you for your kindness."

Past all this, there is an art to ending a conversation. Instead of lingering in prattle and waiting for the world to intervene, make eye contact (if in person), thank the person for the conversation, and then say goodbye. It's that simple, but you must be intentional with your time and direct with your words. As you make your exit, stand tall, feel grounded, and let the connection warm your soul.

MAKE CHOICES WITH CONVICTION

Now that we are witnessing how our stories constantly unfurl and how our communication must be mindfully managed, we can understand the magnitude of the choices we are empowered to make daily.

It's okay to sacrifice an opportunity for the sake of your integrity. If your job doesn't represent reputable clients, they don't do business honestly, or their vision doesn't align with yours – it's all right to say goodbye. What you do says a lot about you.

It's the same with marriages. If it's not working and can't be fixed, it's up to you to determine when it's time to walk away.

You select who you share vital information with. You decide who belongs within the inner fold. And so long as you proceed forward responsibly, mindfully, and compassionately, you can enjoy momentum, understanding, and clarity in life without having to provide proof or explanation to another. You don't have to defend yourself or justify your choices to anyone.

Therefore, it is critical to believe in your best self.

Integrity takes a special kind of bravado – to find your strength to walk a path in what you believe to be kind, just, and true, even when it might cost you. And frankly, there may be no path at all. You might have to blaze your own trail.

Within your choice lies your power.

Approach difficult situations with honest inquiry. If needed, allow yourself time to process. Ask, "Does this decision align with my highest self?" If so, then have it with open-hearted abandon.

STORIES CONNECT US

At the end of the day, we all have stories. And our stories are explicitly separate yet intricately linked.

Every person is living a life as vibrant and complex as your own.

You'll never know the ins and outs of another's life, but:

- They have desires and neuroses, just like you.
- They represent their family and ancestors, just like you.
- They are the product of their environment, just like you.
- They have experienced love and loss, just like you.
- Their existence affects the world around them, just like you.

Stories and experiences can bring others hope, but no one owes you an explanation of their life. No one is required to teach you about their world for you to respect them. You don't have to know another's story to appreciate their journey.

Your sensitivity is your strength.

Only you will ever have the humbling honor of truly knowing your own life, so let this understanding relieve you of the trappings and pitfalls of judging others and yourself.

Mindfully communicate by offering your truth, wholeheartedly connecting with others, and attuning to the world around you. Let love be the language that connects us all.

HONOR YOUR JOURNEY *Recap*

- *Through self-acceptance, you determine your story.*
- *Use the power of the present moment to rewrite your past and craft your future.*
- *Paradigms are widely accepted and relatively undisputed beliefs, yet upon deep personal survey, you may find they contain very little merit.*
- *Self-talk forms your predisposed pace and spiritual space.*
- *The words we use either harm or heal.*
- *Wholehearted communication is truthful, useful, and intentional.*
- *Make your choices with conviction and back yourself.*
- *When you honor the story of another, you cherish the story that you are creating.*

Six

NOTICE YOUR MAGIC

Notice what you notice. Signs, symbols, and synchronicities surround you. Welcome the direction of your Guardian Angels, Spirit Guides, or Inner Guidance. Approach life with childlike wonder. Let yourself be enchanted by everything.

DIVINITY IS EVERYWHERE

You are magic. Your ability to wield your intuitive faculties is not only bona fide and genuine but also your inherent, primordial birthright. And you can access your instinctual insight at any time.

Evidence of your abilities is omnipresent. It's the feeling in the pit of your stomach that detects dishonesty. It's the unexplainable Inner Knowing that directs you past a construction delay. It's the tingle on your arms that lets you know that a loved one (whether alive or passed on) is nearby.

Your intuition knows the answer before the question reveals itself, but it only works if you pay attention.

Try this ten-second meditation to take aligned action:

1. **Pause:** Ground yourself in the present moment.
2. **Breathe:** As you inhale, let your breath fill your belly, hold, and then invite a small smile as you exhale. Feel your confidence crescendo.
3. **Witness:** Observe the world around you and become conscious of your thoughts, emotions, and sensations inside your body.
4. **Trust:** Invite spiritual guidance. If you look, you will see, and then you will know.
5. **Go:** Steered by your intuition, proceed in the direction that feels most aligned to you. Thank the universe for revealing itself.

Thoughts, pulls, and directional markers may continue to repeat. Don't look for the logic; just feel into your body. Sometimes, the "wrong move" is, in fact, in the right direction. Wander, don't wonder. *You* will guide *yourself* via your own personal knowing, and then marvel at your cosmic capability.

When someone reduces an experience to simply "following the signs," they mean that they are intuitively feeling their way along a spiritual path toward universal alignment. They are following the "*hell yeahs*" of the world – the things that light them up, not the stuff that brings them down.

These signs may manifest as little steps in the right direction or result in a giant leap. But with careful thought, you regulate the intensity.

Prepare yourself, though, because true magic promises no time frames, and sometimes signs will take years to reveal their true meaning.

For instance, after deep contemplation, Miles tentatively decides to relocate for a particular job, only to discover that this new city is offering him that and so, so much more. Fast forward a few years, and Miles has met his partner, and together, they have purchased a home and adopted two children – the acceptance of a job transfer spurred all these life upgrades.

Recognizing a sports prodigy, investing in a business, buying a home – all these decisions that have changed many lives began with acknowledging a hunch and taking a risk. Knowing your intuition will help you recognize the signs much more clearly so you can take greater advantage of the opportunities that come your way.

SYMBOLS CONNECT US

Symbols represent objects or ideas, and they convey messages throughout our environment. To the most spiritually adept, symbols convey deeper meanings beneath the obvious. Patterns will emerge, and these synchronicities are telltale indicators that we should *pay attention.*

Symbols become spiritually personal when we are pulled to go beyond what is readily known or seen. They beckon us to link imagery with personal beliefs and experiences.

Symbols can become part of our identities. To some, symbols are entities: Mary the Mother of God, Buddha, Artemis. To others, symbols arise from the ordinary: butterflies, orchids, the color corn-flower blue. But symbols aren't limited to imagery; they can also be sounds, smells, or even flavors. Using metaphor, anything that inspires you can be your own personal symbol.

You'll know that you've identified one of your symbols when you experience a mental pause, almost the stoppage of time. Your body will recalibrate, your mind will clear, and your soul will stir.

Here's how to proclaim your own personal symbols:

1. **Engage:** If you find something that captures your attention, pause and inspect it profoundly. Be aware of how you feel and explore the linkage.
2. **Recreate:** Later, reflect on the symbol that caught your interest. Visualize it, hum it, research it, google it. Get to know it better.
3. **Discover:** Free write about the symbol. What does it mean to you? What personal stories does this symbol evoke?
4. **Declare:** Thank this symbol for making itself known to you. Welcome it into your life and invite it to commune with you as often as you need to be reminded of its meaning.

Afterward, each time you encounter your symbols, you'll feel inspiration, confirmation, and peace simultaneously. Your symbols are divine reminders that the unconscious world around you is col-laborating with your subconscious.

Let the universal spirit fill you!

REVEL IN YOUR MAGIC

When you're just starting to develop your intuitive abilities, you may believe your skills to be coincidences – but there are no such things as coincidences.

It would help if you thought of these flashes of Inner Knowing as downloads; they're up to you to decipher.

Don't lose your sparkle because your powers may not have instant "real world" validation. Magic promises no guaranteed delivery times.

Here are a few ways to witness your magic in action:

- **Join a meditation circle:** You'll sense cocreation and psychic comingling on the deepest levels.
- **Engage in a ritual:** However it manifests for you, a ritual is a way to honor an experience that may otherwise go unnoticed.
- **Spend time in nature:** Getting outside brings us closer to our raw selves. There is peace in the wild.
- **Try something new:** Allow yourself to be guided to a new hobby, something you've never attempted before. What new activities come easily to you? You might surprise yourself!
- **Share your insight:** Say to someone, "I know this seems unrelated, but I had this dream about you," or "I think I have a message for you."
- **Find anything:** The next time you lose something, meditate and see the item in its current location.

- **Stand up for what you believe in:** Find a cause that inflames your spirit and breathe your passion into it. Build a better world.
- **Notice the details:** Walk around the block and leave your phone at home. What do you see and hear that you haven't observed before?
- **Emanate gratefulness:** Take time to appreciate all that surrounds you and all that conspired in your favor to create the one and only you!
- **Self-reflect:** Journal about the lessons you've learned and the innate abilities you sense but have yet to develop fully.

When you start to consider your cosmic insight, you'll discover many ways in which you just *knew* something before you *knew* something. When your confidence grows, your power does, too.

CHILDLIKE WONDERMENT

At one point, when your human life was beginning, you carried no inhibitions when it came to your intuition. Everything was magical. Anything was possible.

Typically, we all show radical psychic powers. But by around age six or seven, we begin to limit ourselves due to societal pressures, kowtowing to the "real world" establishment's parameters and confines. Because, when our abilities are nullified, we learn we fit into the system better.

Until that point, *you are* because you haven't been told *you aren't*.

Within the imagination lies all the potentialities of the universe. Everything around you – everything you see, touch, hear, feel, and taste – starts with imagination.

You still harbor this ability, even if it lies dormant. Society has pressured you to let your conscious mind lead, which means you're not honing in on your subconscious thoughts. Your magic *always* exists within you, although it may currently be a hushed rustle, a light quiver, a flutter deep within – it's still there. The imagination deserves the reverence of a superpower.

Once we learn to acknowledge and work with our subconscious thoughts, our whole world changes.

So, today, be your childlike self again. Watch your favorite movie, read your favorite book, sing your favorite song, or eat your favorite meal. In fact, invite a few kiddos in your life to join in on the festivities. Afterward, take a few minutes to pen a letter to the little you of yesteryear. Thank yourself for all that you did to help create the *you* that you are now.

From this point forward, make every effort to support the innately ingenious, intuitive minds of children. Don't quash their beliefs. Don't tether them to society's accepted version of reality. Don't automatically consent to the human constructs that we've created.

Embolden kids to see the world with wonder, withstanding the temptation of conforming to societal norms. Children are gifted. Play is beneficial. Dreaming is advantageous.

If you've never learned how to process your abilities, you've probably pushed them aside. This may have resulted in you believing you were never able to express yourself wholly. But now you can! Consider this full permission to be a kid again, anytime you want. And feel into every layer of reality.

THE POWER OF AWE

Think of a mermaid sloshing around in her secret underwater grotto of wonder, maintaining a treasure trove of human objects – parasols, candelabras, mirrors – essentially, a library of lore. She caresses a fork and marvels at it, sometimes breaking into song. Mermaids know how to savor our stuff substantially more than we do.

It makes one consider how much we are truly taking for granted daily. Is it possible to be beguiled by the simplest of activities? A jaunt around the block, a pair of socks straight from the dryer, a quick doodle on a page? Could these commonplace examples of the material world be experienced on a deeper dimension?

Absolutely! There is magic in awe, and we can choose to be in awe of anything at any point. This merely requires one to tread the Earth with compassion, acceptance, and intrigue. And, surprisingly, this is a very entertaining way to live.

You look closer. You travel deeper. You savor longer. Your capacity for understanding expands, and you attribute personal meaning to much, much more. The ordinary becomes extraordinary. Colors sharpen. And you learn to fully appreciate something without feeling the need to cage it in language.

With practice, small things that were once one-dimensional – roses, watermelon, marshmallows – now have richness and complexity you were unable to access before.

Ask: **In what ways am I in awe of you?**

And when the big things come your way – for instance, when you stand at the shore of the Pacific Ocean – well, you'll face true planetary scale. Then the choice is yours. Those who don't open their minds will see only as far as the horizon. But for those who use their Inner Knowing, they'll sense the depth, vastness, possibility, and splendor of a breathtaking water world that makes up 70% of Earth's surface ... and, of course, the possibility that mermaids glide around within.

Choose the latter – be in awe and drop to your knees. You'll feel small, and you'll be reminded of the enormous impact of a hundred million tiny decisions and developments that have brought this vision to fruition. You'll fully immerse yourself, exponentially expanding time, turning a moment into a lifetime.

Collect moments like these and not things you don't need. Let the mermaids have those.

The secret to being enchanted by your life is to view the world as both an observer and a participant. Everything – both the big *and* the small – will have great significance. You'll rise above reality and process life in a more meaningful way.

SPIRITUAL GUIDANCE

Your Guardian Angels, or Spirit Guides, are excellent companions. They help you navigate life through your earthly journey. With their help, you'll find your inspiration and creativity amplified.

Who are your guides? You may know your guides in some fashion, or they may be individuals who you've never technically met before.

Your Spirit Guides can manifest as (what we know to be) angels, family ancestors (Grandma), departed loved ones (your dog), ascended masters (Jesus), or famous personalities and historical figures (Betty White). They may even be unknown souls with whom you've had no previous affiliation.

Essentially, their interest is to help psychically support you. They extend their talent, courage, grit, and grace through mystical yet palpable ways. The more you accept and act upon their guidance, the more communication you'll receive.

Here's how to connect with your Spirit Guides:

1. **Meditate:** Access a quiet space and imagine a white light of protection surrounding you.
2. **Visualize:** Walk through the light into an environment where you feel completely at ease. You may find yourself sprawled out on a limb of a childhood apple tree, swaying in a rowboat in a tranquil pond, or surrounded by the din of conversation at the corner table of a coffee shop.

3. **Invite your guide to join you:** Think of their image taking shape near the entrance of your scene; watch them walk toward you across the field, on the dock, or through the door.

4. **Openly connect:** Invite them to join you. Converse about anything and everything. Ask them whatever you want. You don't have to concern yourself with sharing every detail of your life – they're always with you. Listen intently and extend your heart to them.

5. **Express gratitude:** Politely thank them for making themselves available to you. Wish them love and light and say goodbye until next time.

Suppose you haven't identified your Spirit Guide quite yet; complete Steps 1 through 2 above. During Step 3, ask a guide to appear who is in your highest and best interest. The form that steps forward may shock you!

Muster your will to request advice and assistance from your spirit team. Additionally, feel free to use your favorite magical tools to channel your Spirit Guide's support. Ask questions such as: "What cosmic clues will I find today?" and "What lessons are in store for me?"

You'll soon find that this seemingly inner dialogue attunes with external energy. Call on your guides as often as you like to develop your relationship with your Higher Source. There is ethereal support all around you!

SPIRITUAL GROWTH TAKES ACTIVE WORK

In a classic fable, Rabbit challenges Turtle to a footrace. Rabbit, with his alacrity and speed, assumes himself the obvious front-runner. However, Rabbit lets his ego get the best of him. He has no doubt he'll win, so he stops working and takes a nap. And Turtle? Well, in typical fashion, he asserts his one-foot-in-front-of-the-other mentality.

Know that your spiritual journey will take time and bypassing experiences will only hinder your abilities. Although lessons are plentiful in the enlightened realm, we cannot rely on the abridged version of the novel experience. We can't use our spiritual practices to avoid real-life problems. We must process, absorb, and choose to heal, which takes time.

Sometimes a situation will require you to hang around in discomfort, but you are *always* stronger than the circumstances you encounter.

Although life's journey seems long, it's far too short for engaging in effusive gratitude, forcing toxic positivity, offering universal platitudes, dodging complex issues, and/or devoting yourself to energy vampires. Avoid these spiritual pitfalls. You don't owe your spirit to anyone.

No one expects you to be on Cloud Nine all the time. You can't live life in an utter state of harmony, glossing over trauma, and wearing rose-colored glasses. It's simply not possible.

We all encounter trials and tribulations. That's what enriches our journey.

When you work with spirit, you won't always "win." Winning is irrelevant when you're playing at this level. And once you spiritually awaken, you'll feel the pace of life begin to slow as you intensely experience your human existence while growing into your full potential.

So, take the Turtle's pace. There's no need to rush yourself to an unnecessarily early conclusion. Enjoy the natural rhythms and subtle energies as they are revealed to you. Take a step forward. Take a step back. Rest. Reassess. Go your own way. Who knows where you'll end up?

You might be the first to cross the finish line, or you might find yourself on a detour to a woodland hot spring. Either way, savor every step of your journey.

NOTICE YOUR MAGIC *Recap*

- *Your Inner Knowing only works if you pay attention.*
- *Using metaphor, any image that inspires you can be your own personal symbol.*
- *When your confidence grows, your power does, too.*
- *Dreaming, playing, and imagining benefit us as both children and adults.*
- *Awe allows us to fully savor our human experience.*
- *Develop a relationship with your spirit guides to expand your inspiration and creativity.*
- *True spiritual development requires you to process both the good and bad outcomes of your experience.*

Seven

TRUST YOUR SOURCE

"You" are an essential part of "Us," and everything in your life is happening for you, not to you. How are you acting upon the spiritual downloads you are receiving? Embrace the big, gorgeous, luscious unknown.

BIGGER THAN YOU; MORE THAN ME

Aspen trees are heralded for their sophisticated beauty. Tall, erect, assuming trunks are coated in smooth, pale bark with individualized, darkened notches. Their rustling leaves, thin and rounded, transition from green to golden throughout the seasons, displaying a luminous canopy of color.

Each unique tree, with its regal personality, appears to be a proud, separate entity – but it is not! Each Aspen is part of a larger collective, sharing a robust, expansive root structure that links each tree to the others.

Science recognizes a grove of Aspen trees as the largest single organism on Earth, featuring a vast, underground network. This unseen, interconnected landscape can thrive together for thousands of years.

Much like the Aspen trees, we are all connected.

This may seem callous, but it's not about *you*. Life has never been about *you*. Our existence is so much more than one single person can ever be.

Please, feel deeply into these questions, but fear not: **What if there is no *you*? What if there is only *us*?**

This is not to say that you are unimportant. Your existence is essential to the world. You are here for a reason, and that reason is so much bigger than you alone could ever possibly realize yourself to be.

Putting this into perspective: When you speak unkindly to another, you harm yourself. When you deny another food, you starve yourself. When you wage war against another, you battle yourself.

We exist together. We are all one.

Just the reverse is true: When you speak warmly to another, you receive kindness yourself. When you mindfully choose nutritious foods, you feed the collective. When you assert your impassioned purpose, you fuel the world.

Understanding, and thereby accepting, that one is part of the greater whole inspires one to act in favor of the whole. When you work to heal yourself, you help heal the world and all the generations to come after.

When we activate our fullest, most authentic, enlightened selves, we serve the collective. It is our right and our utter responsibility to give the very best of ourselves to provide the very best to everyone. This is reciprocity at its finest.

What you put into the world returns to you; this includes your thoughts, actions, and energies. Every choice you make, no matter how small that choice may seem, affects you as a whole. In turn, those choices alter the world.

This is truly why people can rarely comprehend the impact that they have on history. One seemingly minuscule decision can have compounding effects centuries forward. This isn't mentioned to apply undue pressure; this is simply a reminder that acting in your highest vibration and with your best intention serves the greatest good.

Believing in ourselves, investing in ourselves, benefits all.

THE GLORIOUS GRAY

Imagine that a dense fog has descended upon the trail as you are mountain biking. You can see only a few feet in front of you. You can rely only on your Inner Knowing to lead you forward. This murky, misty space of unknown is called "The Gray."

Total control is an illusion, a mirage, a fantasy. You can't control everything. No one can. Things in life rarely look the way we think they should. And when you bravely take your first leap into new territory or dive into uncharted waters, you may sense some distress, a little fear, or *a lot of fear*. But it's the ambiguity and uncertainty that feels harrowing. It's not the new place, because *where you are* is simply *somewhere* you've yet to explore.

Open yourself to new paths, drift with new paces, shift into new spaces – you never know what riches you may discover.

Now we are hesitant to say that you will find comfort within discomfort. Few of us can confidently approach all situations effortlessly. But, with practice and the proper mindset, you can surefootedly step into the unknown.

You'll always have a stable, reliable foothold when you know yourself and what you stand for.

A gray area exists within every experience: personal, relational, or social. Challenges aren't always clear-cut; the solutions aren't always obvious; the conclusions can't always be rushed. Life is complex and unpredictable.

Everything operates within a spectrum. There is no black or white. And if we learn to sense one another's presence within The Gray – a meeting of souls, if you will – we'd discover that we're never alone.

Sometimes you just don't *know* until you *know*, and then, what you *know* changes based on your own personal journey and evolution.

But *knowing nothing* is distinctly different than *unknowing*. When you *know nothing*, you project a vacancy, a deprivation, an unfulfilled want in your life. When you are *unknowing*, well, then you are opening to a space of infinitesimal potentiality. *Knowing nothing* is perceiving a void; *unknowing* is perceiving a blank canvas.

Push yourself past the known. This may still feel scary – you'll have to admit and be at peace with – how little you actually know. It is within the *unknowing* that enlightenment can emerge.

You can be present within the spaciousness of the unknown. You can embrace the emptiness, the quiet connections. **Does this scare you? Do you feel ungrounded?** Explore this and just be.

You may observe this sensation after being diagnosed with an illness, moving to a new city, or simply entering a room that contains people you've never met before.

Try nourishing yourself with some stabilizing breathwork:

1. **Breathe in:** Inhale through your nose for four seconds, absorbing the fresh oxygen around you.
2. **Steady yourself:** Hold your breath for seven seconds, sensing the fullness of your being.
3. **Let it go:** Exhale from your mouth for eight seconds, allowing your lungs to empty. The complete release of the contents of your lungs exemplifies the surrender of the control that you no longer need.

Within The Gray, you release your reliance on tactics you've devised that have prolonged the illusions of your ego: the security, familiarity, and sureness in your life that's effectively holding you back. But it's time to let go. Amid the ether, you find the will to thrive and reach places you hadn't dared to dream.

SLIPPING BACKWARD

Think about that time when the cartoon character has run off the cliff. He continues to sprint with all his momentum until he catches sight of the ground below. Then he breaks his concentration and plummets back down to the Earth. Talk about a reality check!

We do this to ourselves *all the time*. This is self-sabotage at its strongest.

In real life, this is when you start taking the journey for granted. You feel good, so you stop doing the hard work of maintaining your spiritual practice and sever ties with your Higher Source.

You slip back into your old ways: tossing and turning at night, consuming copious amounts of caffeine, gulping down processed food, and trying to do everything on your own. "Logic" erodes your positive mindset. Your cash flow turns into debt. You make "safe choices," shackling yourself to fear-based jobs, where you take on more responsibility without insisting on fair compensation.

You focus on how miserable you are. You don't stay in the now. You are resentful of the past and worried about the future. You may even begin to experience panic attacks and anxiety. Before you realize it, you imagine – and then expect – everything that can go wrong.

During these spiritual slumps, you need a solid, soulful shake-down.

The company you keep can offer perspective. This fellowship may materialize as an Earth Angel, a life coach, a medium, a priest/priestess, a Soul Squad, a support group, a Spirit Guide, or simply the connected camaraderie of other like-minded individuals.

After all, there is "we" in po*we*r.

Seeking consult can be of great comfort. The advantage of an illuminated perspective outside your own is that it can reaffirm your dreams, highlight the potency of your personal agency, and allow you to focus on your manageable future. You will (gently) be called out on your lies, which helps you see the good you might be overlooking so that you can effectively shatter paradigms holding you back.

You will emerge renewed.

And when your raise your vibrations, your life begins to shift into your ideal personal alignment. It's never the other way around. Your family, your business, your health – it raises or lowers with you, but *it always starts with you*. Fully embrace the present moment, and you will spiritually soar.

BE WHAT YOU WISH TO SEE

It's time to replace the adage "*I'll believe it when I see it*" with "*I'll see it when I believe it*." We're not suggesting being blinded by foolishness; we're talking about projecting a desired outcome and focusing on what you want.

If you are dedicated to your vision and ardently act upon it, then *it shall come to pass.*

Let's put this into perspective: Eva is exhausted during the day. She's rearing a little one while working from home. And when her husband walks through the door each evening after his shift, Eva tosses him the baby. She stomps away in her pajamas, bleating about the to-do list of items that remain undone, the emails that remain unanswered, and the dinner that remains unprepared.

This is the look of disgruntled content, not the essence of an equanimous temperament. Imagine the energetic exchange between the two partners within this environment.

But what if one tiny detail were changed? Instead of inundating a loved one with exasperation, what if we offered them a smile and a kiss hello?

At first, confusion might ensue! But eventually, you'll notice that by channeling your energy in a more positive direction, you'll begin to feel lighter. Your relationship will grow stronger because of these evening greetings, which will set the stage for the rest of the night. There will always be concerns, but setting a high vibrational tone will encourage sincere discussions and straightforward resolutions. By offering love, you will create the conditions for contentment.

The point, after all, isn't about being right – because if that's your goal, you've just effectively flatlined your lifeline. The major takeaway is to discover which actions spiritually fulfill you and live the way that leaves you feeling your best. Resonate feelings of wholeness, show compassion for yourself and those around you, and shift yourself into inner peace. Behold the enlightenment that emerges.

NOTHING IS RANDOM

Imagine a piece of paper haphazardly covered in dots. Those dots seem random, but if you consider the arrangement with intention, you'll be able to connect the scatter with an ink pen, and a complete image will be revealed.

Common sense is heralded in our society, and we have been groomed to believe that many things are left up to chance, that we have no control over casual incidents in our lives, and there is no particular reason one outcome occurs above others. We accept reality as it is. We call this "random."

However, no action is caused by absolute force. Choice guides the results. Sometimes the choices manifest as a long series of seemingly unrelated decisions, but we have always been involved.

How you perceive and manage the world's challenges and blessings is determined by your ability to see and understand life's deeper truths.

The phrase "that's random" is a reactive notion, a coping mechanism, and a way in which we suspend our power. "That's interesting" is proactive, an invitation to explore more deeply, and a reclamation of our intuitive prowess.

"That's interesting" connects you to the moment and uses your knowledge to influence the future.

Since your choices, which brought you to this moment, weren't deliberate, consider the stream of unconscious power that guided your passive actions.

It is theorized that the unconscious is a deep level of connectivity that affects our entire experience. Conversely, our conscious manages our surface-level decision-making, while our subconscious holds our memories, fears, and beliefs. The unconscious is profound, bonding our inner and outer states, linking us to all other beings, all generations that came before us, and all future entities to come.

There is meaning in all events – big and small – if you look hard enough. But the effect of the unconscious and its ability to manifest mind into matter isn't overtly obvious. The only way to understand meaning is to slow down, open up, and pay attention. It takes effort and thoughtfulness to connect the dots in our life. This scope of awareness is the difference between disorderly chaos and magnificent serenity.

TRANSCENDENCE STARTS WITHIN

It's the space within that's the reality of the vessel. Our inner landscapes structure our framework and form, and how we choose to exist within that space ultimately shapes and determines our experiences. Life can feel like your own personal heaven or hell, depending solely upon your perception.

When you are spiritually plugged in, the feeling is absolutely, without-a-doubt, discernible. You sense it throughout your entire being. The crown of your head will reach into the sky, accessing a space of limitless peace and possibility. Your feet will root into the earth beneath you, claiming your space while locking into the world around you. Your heart will lead you forward with gentle, noble strength. This will feel effortlessly regal, like standing in Mountain Pose, floating in placid waters, or sitting upon a royal throne.

Your Inner Knowing is no longer dominated by fear and ego; it is bolstered by intuition, spiritual wisdom, and self-awareness.

You'll wake up, rising with alert tranquility. You'll feel untethered by all that you surmise you should be, have been, and hope to become. You experience a complete undoing of all you thought was once important, rising above the things that don't matter anymore to be the entity of boundless love that you are.

Soulful navigation is noticing the pull of your life's purpose, establishing your personal values, and choosing to navigate the world through your philosophy of life. This is the most earnest way to live, but this journey holds its trials.

In those times when you feel lost or find yourself off course on the fringes, your inner compass will orient you to where you are and tenderly redirect you into alignment. Through your Inner Spirit, you'll always be able to chart a path back home to true self.

WALK FORWARD IN ILLUMINATION

As we walk forward, the world changes and shifts along with us. Nothing remains the same. We can find solace and serenity, making a memory of a moment, just by basking in the splendor surrounding us, especially in the resplendence of the sun and the moon.

The sun urges us to act and to give.

In the sunlight, we soak up the warmth of the sun's rays. Our energy is pure, blissful, and vibrant. There is no hiding from ourselves. Sunlight illuminates everything, both the good and the bad. And as far as the light shines, we count our blessings, enjoy the adventure, and take inspired actions. Following the sun's example, we emit our internal power to shine brightly.

The moon nudges us to rest and to receive.

The moonlight's reflective softness, full of mystery, guides our psychic intuitions. We dive into the watery depths of the moon for higher levels of understanding.

The moon implores you to listen to the whispers of your Inner Voice and surrender completely to heal. Its phases signify constant change. By harnessing your shadow powers (aka the "deficiencies" you've identified in your life), you can now see how they have bolstered your strength and aided your development. The moon encourages you to use your fears to guide you. Trust that you'll be okay. Find the calm in the darkness.

Honor the sun and the moon by making and keeping your promise to them.

- When you wake in the morning, before you leave your bed, close your eyes, and feel the warmth of the sun's rays. Say to yourself, "Like the sun, I rise."
- In the evening, as you turn off the light and drift into slumber, close your eyes, and visualize the comfort of the moon. Say to yourself, "Like the moon, I restore."

These celestial orbs literally illuminate our world; they serve as constant reminders of who we are, and that each new day is a chance to reclaim ourselves and our power. The magnitude of these entities is immense and multitudinous, and they are vital to life on Earth. Their existence is a miracle, and their presence is indispensable! The sun and the moon sustain and support us on a cellular level, but how often do we go about our days without even glancing in their direction?

You are here for a reason. You are not only *enough*, but *so much more*. Like the sun and the moon, you are a life force. Know that your imprint on this world is monumental, meaningful, and significant.

We call this charge "living in faith" versus "living in fear." We focus on everything that can go right, putting our energy toward our cosmic prospects. We've done the work, so it's time to celebrate.

Check in with your true self, consult with your Higher Power, and welcome radical evolution. Most importantly, *simply be you.*

You are meant to live your one precious, luscious life in absolute abundance. You are whole. You are essential. You are loved. And this world needs you.

TRUST YOUR SOURCE *Recap*

- *The thoughts, actions, and energies that you put forth into the world return to you through your relationship with the collective.*
- *Be present within the spaciousness of the unknown.*
- *When you raise your vibrations, your life shifts into your ideal personal alignment.*
- *If you are dedicated to your vision and see it through as much as possible, it shall come to pass.*
- *How you perceive and manage the world's challenges and blessings is determined by your ability to see and understand life's deeper truths.*
- *Our inner landscapes ultimately shape our lives.*
- *Just like the sun and the moon, you are an essential life force.*

CONCLUSION

There is a magical revolution occurring in our world today. Life can often feel bitter, unforgiving, and dangerous, but we still muster the fortitude to show up. What brave souls we are!

We are starting to take back our instinctive power and assert our natural abilities that have been squandered for so long. When we raise our vibrations, we bridge the world of possibility with everyday "reality." Our personal magic may not instantly right the wrongs of the world, but it can empower us to create the change we wish to see.

Magic permeates your life, whether you are asserting your gifts or not. Magic is all around you. You can't escape its influence. You can choose not to wield its power, but why would you abandon your birthright?

The Magic Within was written as a guide to unleash the radiant energy you contain within you, full of enlightened essays and exercises. We implore you to do the work, access your intuition, and enjoy the journey of self-discovery. It is our earnest hope that you will feel into the flow of *The Magic Within* and sense the gradual expansion of "I can't" to "I can" to "I am."

Should you reread *The Magic Within*, you'll experience it entirely on another level, indicative of your spiritual growth. The words within these pages may remain the same, but your personal definition of the text will continue to evolve.

Life is dynamic, complex, and nuanced, and how you view the world, along with how you'll use the insight within this book, will depend upon your current experience within the world.

Through wounded souls and harmed egos, we open our hearts – fully, vulnerably, and completely – and thus, life emerges as a more meaningful experience.

Now, let it all go. All that you've learned, all that you know. Release the need to be anything at all. Be at one with your body, soul, and mind.

Emanate joy, kindness, and understanding.

Exhale.

Still extending all the love in the universe,

Kara & Britt

ACKNOWLEDGMENTS

We have felt uplifted and supported throughout every stage of *The Magic Within*, its contents long in the works before we even realized they would be transcribed in tangible form. We treasure our families and friends for their everlasting love and for the life-changing impact they have had and continue to have on our lives.

It is with appreciation that we especially mention author and attorney Rocco Cozza for his invaluable guidance. We thank our editors, Larry Butler and Kristin Campbell for their eagle-eyed discernment, and our talented cover designer, Wonderbug Creations. We are indebted to the chipper caffeine-slogging baristas at our local coffee shop for their encouraging presence during our long work sessions.

And lastly, we humbly extend sincere gratitude to our collective of "First Readers," who took the time to review *The Magic Within* during its very early, infantile stages. Their invaluable insight has helped shape and refine this project into what it is today. We wholeheartedly thank them for their endless enthusiasm, encouragement, and commitment.

Above all else, we long to offer special acknowledgment to our husbands, children, and housemates who have helped sustain our late-night work sessions and countless get-togethers. They have been a significant source of stories, lessons, and epiphanies. They truly make our worlds all the more magical.

—

To Justin, my husband, my rock: Babe, meeting you was a stroke of serendipity. We both found ourselves in a place we hadn't planned, yet our meeting was kismet. This is what happens when you follow your heart and not the plan. From then on, you would be one of the main characters in my life story. Through our love, I was able to fix what was broken inside me. I'm not sure if I would have if it weren't for you in my life. Thank you for your endless love.

To Calum, my first Earth Angel, who has always shown me unconditional love: I'll never forget the moment you said to me, "You are stronger than you think you are. You are capable of anything." Cal, you believed in me before I believed in myself. You inspire me to be my true authentic self.

To Ethan, my sidekick and the boy who is wise beyond his years: At age eight, you told me, "You push yourself out of your comfort zone until that becomes your new comfort zone." You motivate me. Thank you for accepting me for me.

You all fill my heart with so much love. Thank you.

Kara

—

To my adorable husband, Colby: You are my biggest source of strength. Thank you for always seeing the best in me. I look forward to our analog RV years ahead as we sink deeper into nature together.

To Penn, my little man, who is always quick to crack a joke and make me smile: You're an old soul, and I can only hope that you are learning as much from me as I am learning from you. You remind me to stay true to myself, and should I ever feel like I don't fit in, it's time to break the mold.

And to Luna, my forever pup: You have taught me that one should never apologize for taking up space, and it's our duty to fully appreciate the treats life hands us.

I love, love, love you all.

Britt

Kara Evans: Ever since Kara was a little girl, she experienced visions and received messages that she didn't quite understand and that others seemingly could not see. She always knew that there was more to this world. Kara has a way of reaching out to those in spiritual need, believing in them more than they believe in themselves and wanting to bring out the very best in people. She knows, from experience, that no matter how toxic life can be, one should never lose faith in themselves.

Born in Omaha, NE, and raised in Kansas City, MO, Kara attended the University of Missouri - Kansas City. She has built her career by leveraging her expertise in corporate staffing and information technology. Over the past decade, she started her spiritual side business and passion project – Reiki & Readings (R&R).

Kara lives in Canonsburg, PA, with her family, and their Coton de Tuléar, Sybil, keeps things interesting around the house. You can learn more about Kara at: www.karaevansspiritualhealer.com.

—

Britt Schelling: Inspired by a magical, creative, wild-hearted family, Britt has always felt called to be a changemaker. She was raised barefoot in the Laurel Highlands mountains, south of Pittsburgh, Pennsylvania and attended Louisiana State University.

As an employee and volunteer in the social sector for many years, Britt is a staunch activist for human rights, mental health care, and domestic violence awareness. She believes everyone harbors within them a unique, fascinating, and affecting story.

When Britt isn't ferociously creating on her MacBook, she's deep in the woodlands on yet another hiking trail. Britt lives in Peters Township, Pennsylvania, with her husband, son, and mischievous Weimaraner. You can learn more about Britt's projects at: www.abrittdifferent.com.